AROUND THE WORLD IN 50 WAYS

WRITTEN BY
DAN SMITH

ILLUSTRATED BY
FRANCES CASTLE

HOW TO USE THIS BOOK

HI, MY NAME'S ZAK. WELCOME TO *AROUND THE WORLD IN 50 WAYS.* IF YOU THINK THIS IS A BOOK WHERE YOU OPEN AT PAGE 1 AND READ RIGHT THROUGH TO THE END, THEN THINK AGAIN.

IN THIS BOOK, **YOU** ARE THE MAIN CHARACTER. THE AIM IS TO TAKE A TRIP AROUND THE WORLD, STARTING AND ENDING IN LONDON.

YOU'RE IN CHARGE HERE, SO YOU CHOOSE WHERE TO GO AND WHAT TO DO NEXT!

YOU'LL VISIT INCREDIBLE CITIES ALONG THE WAY AND TRY THINGS YOU'VE NEVER DONE BEFORE. NOW'S YOUR CHANCE TO SURF IN HONOLULU, RIDE A CAMEL IN MARRAKECH, SNORKEL IN QUEENSLAND, OR TAKE A TAXI IN NEW YORK.

THERE ARE MANY DIFFERENT WAYS TO GET FROM A TO B. YOU'LL TAKE PLANE RIDES, OF COURSE, BUT EVER BEEN IN A TUK-TUK, A BICYCLE RICKSHAW, OR A JEEPNEY? THIS IS WHERE YOU GET TO HAVE FUN!

YOUR TRIP IS GUARANTEED TO BE GREAT FUN EVEN WHEN IT GOES WRONG! GO BACK TO THE BEGINNING AND HAVE A COMPLETELY DIFFERENT ADVENTURE. JUST KEEP GOING UNTIL YOU FIND THE RIGHT PATH.

SO, ARE YOU READY TO JOIN ME ON THE TRIP OF A LIFETIME? THEN STOP HANGING AROUND!

TURN THE PAGE AND LET'S BEGIN...

PICK THE RIGHT ROUTE AND YOU'LL MAKE IT ALL THE WAY AROUND THE PLANET AND SAFELY BACK TO LONDON. BUT BE WARNED, TAKE A WRONG TURN, AND YOUR JOURNEY WILL COME TO A...

DEAD END!

IF IT DOES, DON'T PANIC!

GO TO P6

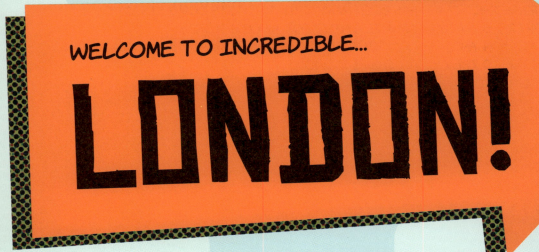

WELCOME TO INCREDIBLE...
LONDON!

OUR JOURNEY STARTS IN LONDON, CAPITAL OF THE UK AND ONE OF THE WORLD'S MOST EXCITING CITIES. THERE'S SOMETHING FOR EVERYONE HERE – MUSIC, ART, HISTORY, THEATER, SPORTS, AND FABULOUS FOOD! WE MIGHT SEE THE QUEEN AT BUCKINGHAM PALACE, TAKE A BOAT RIDE ON THE THAMES, COZY UP WITH DINOSAURS AT THE NATURAL HISTORY MUSEUM, OR CATCH A WEST-END SHOW, ALL BEFORE BEDTIME!

THE TOWER

FIRST STOP. THE TOWER OF LONDON, BUILT BY WILLIAM THE CONQUEROR IN 1066. THE TOWER HAS BEEN MANY THINGS IN ITS LONG HISTORY – A FORTRESS, A ROYAL PALACE, A MINT FOR MAKING MONEY, A PRISON, AND EVEN A ZOO! TODAY, IT'S HOME TO THE CROWN JEWELS – WOW!

WHERE NEXT?

TIME TO MAKE YOUR FIRST CHOICE. WHICH OPTION WILL YOU TAKE TO CONTINUE YOUR JOURNEY?

TAKE A TRAIN
GO TO P40

TAKE A BUS
GO TO P122

TAKE A BOAT
GO TO P8

LEGEND HAS IT THE TOWER WILL FALL IF THE RAVENS THAT LIVE THERE EVER FLY AWAY.

7

SAIL AWAY ON A...
CRUISE SHIP

WE'VE MADE IT TO THE COAST AND BOARDED AN OCEAN LINER. OUR CABIN HAS A PERFECT VIEW OF THE DEEP BLUE SEA, SO THERE'S NO CHANCE OF GETTING BORED! THIS MEGA-SHIP IS LIKE A FLOATING CITY. WE CAN EAT AT A DIFFERENT RESTAURANT EVERY DAY, WHOOSH DOWN WATERSLIDES INTO A HEATED SWIMMING POOL, CATCH A SHOW AT THE ON-BOARD THEATER, OR EVEN STROLL ON DECK THROUGH THE SHIP'S OWN TREE-LINED PARK.

THE WORLD'S MOST EXPENSIVE CABIN, ON BOARD *QUEEN MARY 2* INCLUDES HIS AND HERS BATHROOMS, A PRIVATE DECK, AND A GYM! I'M AFRAID YOUR CABIN WILL BE A LITTLE MORE BASIC.

OASIS OF THE SEAS

THE BIGGEST CRUISE SHIP IN THE WORLD HAS ENOUGH SPACE FOR ALMOST 7,000 PASSENGERS AND OVER 2,000 CREW. IT TAKES ABOUT 220 COOKS JUST TO KEEP EVERYBODY FED. EACH WEEK, THE KITCHEN COOKS UP 85,000 EGGS, ABOUT 16,000 LB (7,250 KG) OF CHICKEN, AND 18,000 SLICES OF PIZZA. YOU WON'T GO HUNGRY!

1 DAY EAST
GO TO P72

4 DAYS WEST
GO TO P156

WHERE NEXT?

EAST OR WEST? WHICH WAY WILL YOU GO AND HOW LONG WILL YOU STAY ON BOARD?

WUPPERTAL!

WE'VE MADE IT TO WUPPERTAL, A CITY IN THE GERMAN COUNTRYSIDE FAMOUS FOR ITS SUSPENSION RAILWAY. THE RAILWAY – CALLED *SCHWEBEBAHN* IN GERMAN AND NICKNAMED "THE STEELY DRAGON" – HAS BEEN MOVING PEOPLE AROUND THE CITY SINCE 1901. WITH 20 STATIONS ALONG ITS ROUTE, THE MONORAIL IS NOT ONLY A GREAT WAY TO GET AROUND THE CITY, IT HELPS KEEP THE ROADS BELOW FREE OF TRAFFIC JAMS.

OH NO! THERE'S BEEN A POWER SURGE, AND YOUR TRAIN IS STUCK BETWEEN STATIONS! YOUR JOURNEY HAS GROUND TO A HALT, BUT AT LEAST THE VIEWS ARE GOOD. HANG AROUND FOR THE ENGINEER TO FIX THE TRAIN, AND THEN GO BACK TO LONDON TO START YOUR ADVENTURE AGAIN.

DEAD END!

03

CHIANG MAI!

WE'VE ARRIVED IN NORTHERN THAILAND'S MOST IMPORTANT CITY. FOLLOW ME THROUGH THE BACKSTREETS OF THE CITY CENTER – IT'S A TOTAL MAZE! CHIANG MAI MEANS "NEW CITY," THOUGH IT WAS FOUNDED IN 1296 (ON THE SITE OF AN EVEN OLDER CITY!) AND WAS THE CAPITAL OF THE ANCIENT "LAN NA" KINGDOM.

UH OH! THE CITY IS SURROUNDED BY A MOAT. WHEN WE REACH IT, WE'RE FORCED BACK INTO THE TWISTY BACKSTREETS! WE'LL NEVER FIND OUR WAY OUT OF HERE TONIGHT. OUR JOURNEY IS AT AN END – MIGHT AS WELL TRY A SPICY LEMONGRASS SAUSAGE BEFORE WE HEAD BACK TO LONDON TO START OUR ADVENTURE AGAIN.

WAT CHIANG MAN

THE CITY IS HOME TO MORE THAN 300 BUDDHIST TEMPLES AND WAT CHIANG MAN IS THE OLDEST OF THEM ALL. THE KING LIVED HERE WHEN THE CITY WAS BUILT BACK IN THE 13TH CENTURY. CHIANG MAN MEANS "CITY STABLE," BUT A STABLE FOR WHAT? MAYBE THE LIFE-SIZE STONE ELEPHANTS AT THE BASE OF THE MAIN BUILDING ARE A CLUE?

DEAD END!

CHIANG MAI IS HOME TO DOI INTHANON, THAILAND'S HIGHEST MOUNTAIN.

13

DISCOVER QUIRKY...
REYKJAVÍK!

I CAN'T WAIT TO SHOW YOU REYKJAVÍK, THE CAPITAL OF ICELAND AND THE MOST NORTHERLY CAPITAL CITY IN THE WORLD. THE LOCALS ARE VERY PROUD OF THEIR COASTAL METROPOLIS, AND I CAN SEE WHY! THE ARCHITECTURE IS UNIQUE, AND THERE ARE AMAZING OUTDOOR SWIMMING POOLS, COOL CAFÉS (I HOPE YOU LIKE FISH!), AND WHALE WATCHING!

HOT SPRINGS

REYKJAVÍK MEANS "SMOKY BAY." THE CITY TAKES ITS NAME FROM THE STEAM THAT RISES FROM THE MANY HOT SPRINGS. THE MOST FAMOUS IS THE BLUE LAGOON.

WHERE NEXT?

IT'S A HARD PLACE TO LEAVE, BUT WE NEED TO BE ON OUR WAY!

FLY 9 HRS

GO TO P114

FLY 14 HRS

GO TO P56

THE NORTHERN LIGHTS

ONE OF THE HIGHLIGHTS OF ANY TRIP TO ICELAND IS THE CHANCE TO SEE THE NORTHERN LIGHTS – A BALLET OF BEAUTIFUL GREEN LIGHT THAT DANCES ACROSS THE SKY ON CLEAR WINTER NIGHTS. THE LIGHTS (ALSO KNOWN AS AURORA BOREALIS) ARE CAUSED BY COLLISIONS BETWEEN ELECTRICALLY CHARGED PARTICLES FROM THE SUN AS THEY ENTER THE EARTH'S ATMOSPHERE. YOU WON'T BELIEVE YOUR EYES!

ULAANBAATA

ALLOW ME TO SHOW YOU AROUND MONGOLIA'S CAPITAL CITY. IT'S VERY DIFFERENT FROM THE REST OF THIS HUGE COUNTRY, WHICH IS FULL OF WIDE OPEN SPACES, GRASSLANDS, MOUNTAINS, AND DESERT. HOME TO ALMOST HALF OF THE POPULATION, ULAANBAATAR IS A HUSTLING, BUSTLING CITY, BUZZING WITH EXCITEMENT AND SOMETIMES A BIT CHAOTIC!

THE GENGHIS KHAN STATUE

LET'S CHECK OUT ONE OF MONGOLIA'S MOST SPECTACULAR SITES – A GIANT STATUE OF GENGHIS KHAN ON HORSEBACK. GENGHIS KHAN WAS THE LEADER OF THE MONGOL PEOPLE ABOUT EIGHT CENTURIES AGO. A FEARSOME WARRIOR, HE CONQUERED AN EMPIRE THAT STRETCHED ACROSS ASIA AND INTO EUROPE – THE BIGGEST EMPIRE ANYONE HAS EVER RULED! OLD GENGHIS IS STILL REGARDED AS THE GREATEST HERO IN THE COUNTRY'S HISTORY.

R!

WHERE NEXT?

ENOUGH HORSING AROUND!
IT'S TIME TO SAY GOODBYE
TO GENGHIS KHAN – WE HAVE
A PLANE TO CATCH.

FLY 13 HRS

GO TO **P44**

FLY 10 HRS

GO TO **P136**

THE STATUE, UNVEILED IN 2008,
IS THE BIGGEST STATUE OF A
HORSE ANYWHERE AND MEASURES
AN INCREDIBLE 131 FT (40 M) TALL.

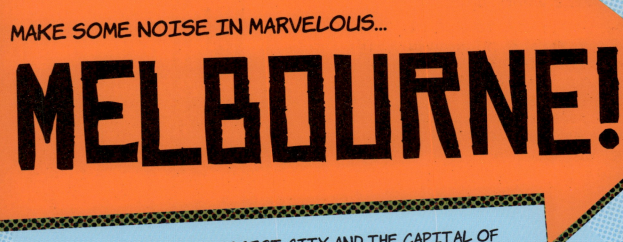

MAKE SOME NOISE IN MARVELOUS...

MELBOURNE!

AUSTRALIA'S SECOND-BIGGEST CITY AND THE CAPITAL OF THE STATE OF VICTORIA, MELBOURNE IS RATED ONE OF THE BEST PLACES TO LIVE IN THE WORLD. THERE'S LOADS TO DO AND SEE – JUMP ABOARD A HERITAGE RAILWAY, VISIT ONE OF THE AWESOME AMUSEMENT PARKS OR THE AQUARIUM. BUT IF SPORTS ARE MORE YOUR THING – AND MELBURNIANS LOVE THEIR SPORTS – WE COULD WATCH AN AUSSIE RULES FOOTBALL GAME AT THE LEGENDARY MELBOURNE CRICKET GROUND.

THE MELBOURNE CUP

THE CITY IS HOME TO ANOTHER OF THE WORLD'S GREAT SPORTING EVENTS – THE MELBOURNE CUP HORSE RACE. FIRST HELD IN 1861, IT IS RUN OVER TWO MILES AT THE CITY'S FLEMINGTON RACECOURSE. HORSES COME FROM AROUND THE GLOBE TO COMPETE, AND EVERY YEAR THE WHOLE CITY STOPS TO SEE WHO WILL WIN.

WHERE NEXT?

GIDDYUP THERE OR YOU'LL MISS YOUR NEXT FLIGHT!

FLY 9 HRS 30 MINS

GO TO P160

FLY 3 HRS 30 MINS

GO TO P104

PREPARE FOR A BUMPY RIDE IN A...
JEEP

ONE JEEP WAS AWARDED A PURPLE HEART – AN AMERICAN MILITARY MEDAL – FOR ITS SERVICE IN THE SECOND WORLD WAR.

WE'VE GOT A ROCKY ROAD AHEAD OF US, SO LET'S LEAP INTO A JEEP. THESE TOUGH LITTLE VEHICLES WERE FIRST USED TO CARRY TROOPS DURING THE SECOND WORLD WAR. THEY COULD DO ANYTHING AND GO ANYWHERE, WHICH MADE THEM PERFECT FOR TRANSPORTING SOLDIERS IN PLACES WHERE THE ROADS WERE BAD OR TOO DANGEROUS FOR ORDINARY CARS.

GP VEHICLES?

NO ONE KNOWS FOR SURE HOW THE JEEP GOT ITS NAME, BUT ONE THEORY IS THAT THE EARLIEST JEEPS WERE KNOWN AS "GENERAL PURPOSE" OR "GP" VEHICLES. BECAUSE GP IS A BIT OF A MOUTHFUL, THE NICKNAME "JEEP" WAS BORN!

WHERE NEXT?

HOW LONG CAN YOU HANDLE THESE ROUGH ROADS? CHOOSE THE LENGTH OF YOUR JOURNEY...

21 HRS

GO TO P52

13 HRS

GO TO P142

MOSCOW!

OVER 6 MILLION PEOPLE VISIT RED SQUARE EVERY YEAR

PREPARE TO SPEND A DAY IN MOSCOW WALKING THROUGH RUSSIAN HISTORY! FOLLOW ME, AND WE'LL UNRAVEL THE CITY'S MEDIEVAL PAST. WE'LL VISIT GORKY PARK, TAKE IN A PUPPET SHOW, AND VISIT THE COSMONAUTICS MUSEUM. BUT FIRST, LET'S START OUR DAY IN THE HEART OF THIS MAJESTIC CITY BY VISITING RED SQUARE AND THE KREMLIN – THE CITY'S FOUNDING FORTRESS.

ST. BASIL'S CATHEDRAL

THIS CRAZY CONFUSION OF COLORS, PATTERNS, AND SHAPES IS IN A STYLE THAT IS UNIQUE TO RUSSIAN ARCHITECTURE. ITS NINE DOMES REPRESENT FLAMES RISING INTO THE SKY.

WHERE NEXT?

TIME TO GO! HOW WILL YOU LEAVE MOSCOW – BY AIR OR OVERLAND?

TAKE A TRAIN
GO TO P34

TAKE A PLANE
GO TO P46

ANTARCTICA!

ANTARCTICA IS THE MOST SOUTHERLY CONTINENT ON EARTH AND IN THE MIDDLE OF IT IS THE SOUTH POLE. BOY, IS IT COLD! ABOUT 90 PERCENT OF ALL THE ICE ON THE PLANET IS HERE, SO YOU'LL UNDERSTAND WHY WE NEED TO WRAP UP WARM – THE ICE IS MORE THAN 2.5 MI (4 KM) THICK IN SOME PLACES! THE FIRST EXPLORERS ONLY REACHED HERE IN 1911, AND EVEN TODAY, ONLY ABOUT 1,000 SCIENTISTS LIVE HERE, IN SPECIAL RESEARCH STATIONS.

LET'S WATCH THE EMPEROR PENGUINS – DON'T GET TOO CLOSE THOUGH. UH OH! DID YOU HEAR THAT CRACKING SOUND? THE ICE IS TOO THIN – IT'S BREAKING UP AND WE'RE STRANDED! LET'S HOPE A RESEARCH SHIP COMES ALONG SOON. BACK TO THE START WE GO.

DEAD END!

ALTHOUGH THERE'S LOADS OF ICE, ANTARCTICA IS OFFICIALLY A DESERT BECAUSE IT HARDLY EVER RAINS.

GUATEMALA

HOW ABOUT A TOUR AROUND GUATEMALA CITY, CAPITAL OF THE REPUBLIC OF GUATEMALA? BURSTING OUT OF A MOUNTAIN VALLEY, THIS IS NO PLACE FOR THE FAINTHEARTED. IT'S BUSTLING, BIG, AND NOISY, BUT WITH SOMEONE TO SHOW YOU WHERE TO GO, YOU'LL DISCOVER THIS IS A REALLY FRIENDLY TOWN.

CITY

HOP ON A CHICKEN BUS

THERE'S NO BETTER PLACE TO GO EXPLORING THAN THE HUGE CENTRAL MARKET, WHICH IS FULL OF STALLS SELLING FLOWERS, FOOD, AND GUATEMALAN HANDICRAFTS. WE'LL TAKE A CHICKEN BUS TO GET THERE. DON'T WORRY, YOU WON'T HAVE TO SHARE YOUR SEAT WITH AN ACTUAL CHICKEN! THESE ARE OLD SCHOOL BUSES REDECORATED IN CRAZY, BRIGHT DESIGNS. THEY MIGHT NOT BE THE MOST COMFORTABLE, BUT YOU'RE SURE TO REMEMBER THE RIDE!

WHERE NEXT?

HAD ENOUGH OF PLAYING CHICKEN? LET'S GET OUT OF HERE. THE AIRPORT'S ONLY 20 MINUTES AWAY, BY BUS!

FLY 2 HRS 10 MINS
GO TO P102

FLY 24 HRS
GO TO P120

GUATEMALA HAS 29 ACTIVE VOLCANOES, SO WATCH OUT FOR AN ERUPTION!

TAKE TO THE AIR IN AN...
AIRBUS A320

DO YOU WANT AN AISLE SEAT, OR TO SIT NEXT TO THE WINDOW SO YOU CAN LOOK OUT AS WE SKIM ACROSS THE CLOUDS?

SINCE A320S STARTED FLYING IN 1988, THEY HAVE MADE OVER 100 MILLION FLIGHTS CARRYING OVER 10 BILLION PASSENGERS. IT'S OFFICIALLY THE WORLD'S MOST POPULAR PASSENGER AIRPLANE.

ON BOARD

PEOPLE CAN BE SUPERSTITIOUS, SO THERE ISN'T A ROW 13 ON BOARD SOME OF THESE PLANES. I'M IN ROW 14 – TIME TO SETTLE DOWN AND WATCH A MOVIE BEFORE DINNER!

WHERE NEXT?

BUCKLE UP, IT'S TIME FOR TAKEOFF. SHORT-HAUL OR LONG-HAUL? YOU DECIDE.

2 HRS 30 MINS

GO TO P22

AN AIRBUS A320 TAKES OFF OR LANDS SOMEWHERE IN THE WORLD EVERY 2.5 SECONDS OF EVERY DAY.

9 HRS 40 MINS

GO TO P112

IT'S CARNIVAL TIME IN...

RIO DE JANEIRO!

JOIN ME IN THE WORLD'S GREATEST PARTY CITY. ENJOY AN UNFORGETTABLE CARNIVAL AS WE SWAY TO THE SOUNDS OF SAMBA AND BOOGIE TO THE BOSSA NOVA BEATS. WHEN WE'RE HUNGRY, WE'LL STOP OFF FOR A BOWL OF FEIJOADA – A DELICIOUS PORK-AND-BLACK-BEAN STEW THAT THE LOCALS LOVE.

GUARDIAN OF THE CITY

WE COULD TAKE THE RACK RAILWAY UP NEARBY CORCOVADO MOUNTAIN AND EXPLORE THE GIANT STATUE OF CHRIST THE REDEEMER THAT OVERLOOKS THE CITY. THEN PERHAPS HEAD DOWN TO COPACABANA, THE FAMOUS BEACH BY THE ATLANTIC OCEAN. IT'S THE PERFECT PLACE TO SUNBATHE, PLAY BEACH SOCCER, OR JUST WATCH THE WORLD GO BY.

WHERE NEXT?

HAD ENOUGH DANCING? LET'S GET OUT OF HERE. DO WE SAIL OR FLY?

TAKE A BOAT
GO TO P110

CATCH A PLANE
GO TO P128

IN 1950, THE WORLD CUP SOCCER FINAL AT RIO'S MARACANÃ STADIUM WAS WATCHED BY THE LARGEST CROWD EVER – 173,850 PEOPLE!

NAIROBI!

NAIROBI, THE CAPITAL OF KENYA, HAS COME A LONG WAY SINCE IT WAS ESTABLISHED AS A TRAIN DEPOT IN 1899. THESE DAYS, IT'S A BUSY CITY, FULL OF AMAZING PLACES TO VISIT, LIKE KARURA FOREST OR NAIROBI SNAKE PARK. SOME OF THE BEST ARTISTS AND MUSICIANS IN AFRICA LIVE HERE, AND THE FOOD IS GREAT, TOO. I RECOMMEND GOAT STEW AND *UGALI* – A SORT OF DOUGHY PORRIDGE. YUM!

NAIROBI NATIONAL PARK

WE CAN'T LEAVE WITHOUT VISITING NAIROBI NATIONAL PARK – THIS IS THE ONLY LARGE CITY IN THE WORLD WITH ITS OWN BIG–GAME RESERVE. JUST A SHORT HOP FROM ALL THOSE SKYSCRAPERS AND BUSTLING STREETS, WE'LL SEE LIONS, GIRAFFES, ZEBRAS, BABOONS, CHEETAHS, AND BLACK RHINOS GOING ABOUT THEIR DAILY LIVES IN THEIR INCREDIBLE NATURAL HABITAT.

WHERE NEXT?

TIME TO GO TO JOMO KENYATTA INTERNATIONAL AIRPORT AND TAKE THE NEXT FLIGHT OUT.

FLY 4 HRS
GO TO P158

FLY 6 HRS
GO TO P56

BLACK RHINOS ARE EXTREMELY RARE – THERE ARE ONLY ABOUT 5,000 LEFT IN THE WORLD.

TRANS-SIBERIAN RAILWAY!

WELCOME TO YOUR HOME FOR THE NEXT FEW DAYS! LIKE MOST PEOPLE TRAVELING ON THE TRANS-SIBERIAN, WE'RE BUNKING IN A FOUR-BERTH SLEEPER CABIN.

WHERE NEXT?

THE JOURNEY ACROSS THE SIBERIAN WILDERNESS IS AMAZING – HOW LONG WILL YOU STAY ON BOARD?

6 DAYS
GO TO **P16**

7 DAYS
GO TO **P140**

LAKE BAIKAL

THE TRAIN IS ON ITS WAY AROUND THE SHORES OF LAKE BAIKAL, THE OLDEST AND DEEPEST LAKE IN THE WORLD. IT PLUNGES TO OVER 5,000 FT (1,637 M) AND HOLDS ONE-FIFTH OF ALL THE WORLD'S FRESH WATER. WOW!

THREE DRIVERS ARE NEEDED FOR THE TRIP ACROSS RUSSIA, WORKING IN ROTATION.

TIME TO EXPLORE...
LAHORE!

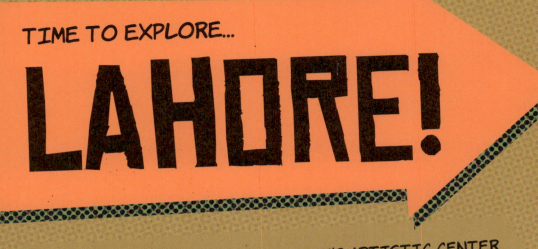

WE'VE ARRIVED IN LAHORE, PAKISTAN'S ARTISTIC CENTER AND SECOND-BIGGEST CITY AFTER KARACHI. AS WE MOVE THROUGH THE STREETS, DIFFERENT PARTS OF LAHORE'S LONG HISTORY COME TO LIFE. MY FAVORITE AREA IS THE WALLED OLD CITY. LET'S TAKE A TANGA THERE — ONE OF THE HORSE-DRAWN CARRIAGES THAT HAVE TRANSPORTED LOCALS FOR CENTURIES. IT MIGHT NOT BE THE QUICKEST WAY TO TRAVEL, BUT IT'S CHEAP, THE VIEWS ARE GREAT, AND THE GENTLE CLATTER OF HORSES' HOOVES MAKES A NICE CHANGE FROM THE NOISY TRAFFIC.

DEAD END!

LOLLYWOOD

THE PAKISTANI FILM INDUSTRY IS BASED IN LAHORE AND IS NICKNAMED "LOLLYWOOD." WHAT'S THAT? THEY WANT US TO STAR IN THE LATEST ACTION MOVIE? AMAZING! THIS IS NO TIME TO LEAVE. WE'LL HAVE TO STAY FOR SIX MONTHS, THEN START OUR TRIP ALL OVER AGAIN FROM LONDON ONCE FILMING IS COMPLETE. ACTION!

GLIDE THROUGH GLORIOUS...
VENICE!

VENICE, THE JEWEL OF NORTHERN ITALY, IS LIKE NOWHERE ELSE. THE CITY IS MADE UP OF OVER 100 SMALL ISLANDS CONNECTED BY BRIDGES AND CANALS, SO IT FEELS LIKE IT'S AFLOAT. WHEREVER YOU TURN, YOU'LL FIND A BEAUTIFUL BUILDING, NONE MORE SO THAN THE AMAZING ST. MARK'S BASILICA ON THE FAMOUS PIAZZA SAN MARCO. BEWARE THOUGH – ON A HOT DAY, THE CANALS CAN GET A LITTLE BIT STINKY!

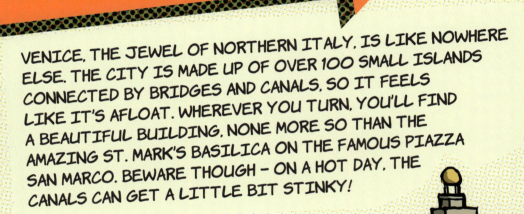

TAKE A SLOW GONDOLA

THERE REALLY IS ONLY ONE WAY TO SEE VENICE, SO LET'S JUMP ON BOARD A GONDOLA. IT'S A BANANA-SHAPED ROWING BOAT WITH A FLAT BOTTOM THAT IS PERFECT FOR GETTING AROUND THE MAZE OF CANALS. A GONDOLIER STANDS AT THE BACK OF THE BOAT AND PUSHES IT ALONG WITH A LONG POLE. WE CAN RELAX AND TAKE IN THE SIGHTS WHILE THE GONDOLIER DOES ALL THE HARD WORK.

WHERE NEXT?

IT'S TIME TO SAY
ARRIVEDERCI, OR GOODBYE,
TO VENICE. WHICH FLIGHT
WILL YOU TAKE?

FLY 8 HRS DRIVE 2 HRS
GO TO P138

FLY 4 HRS 15 MINS
GO TO P154

GONDOLAS WERE FIRST USED IN
VENICE A THOUSAND YEARS AGO.

TICKETS, PLEASE! ALL ABOARD THE...

EUROSTAR

WE ARE ON BOARD ONE OF THE 400 EUROSTAR TRAINS THAT SHUTTLE PASSENGERS AND VEHICLES BACK AND FORTH BETWEEN THE UK AND MAINLAND EUROPE EVERY DAY. THE TRAINS PASS THROUGH THE CHANNEL TUNNEL, WHICH RUNS FOR 23.5 MI (38 KM) BENEATH THE ENGLISH CHANNEL.

THE TUNNEL

THE IDEA FOR A CHANNEL TUNNEL WAS FIRST SUGGESTED IN 1802 BUT IT WASN'T UNTIL 1988 THAT CONSTRUCTION BEGAN. THE TUNNEL WAS OPENED SIX YEARS LATER AND IS THE LONGEST UNDERSEA TUNNEL IN THE WORLD.

WHERE NEXT?

GOODBYE LONDON AND HELLO MAINLAND EUROPE! BUT AS WE SPEED TOWARDS THE CHANNEL TUNNEL, WHICH WAY WILL WE GO?

TRAVEL 2 HRS 15 MINS
GO TO P130

TRAVEL 2 HRS
GO TO P62

OVER A MILLION PET CATS AND DOGS HAVE TRAVELED ON THE EUROSTAR!

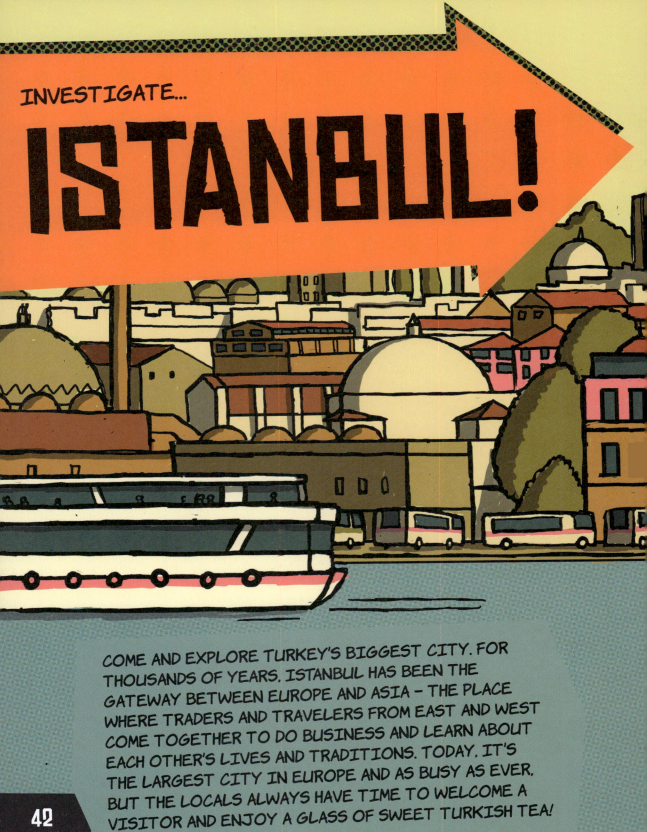

INVESTIGATE...
ISTANBUL!

COME AND EXPLORE TURKEY'S BIGGEST CITY. FOR THOUSANDS OF YEARS, ISTANBUL HAS BEEN THE GATEWAY BETWEEN EUROPE AND ASIA – THE PLACE WHERE TRADERS AND TRAVELERS FROM EAST AND WEST COME TOGETHER TO DO BUSINESS AND LEARN ABOUT EACH OTHER'S LIVES AND TRADITIONS. TODAY, IT'S THE LARGEST CITY IN EUROPE AND AS BUSY AS EVER, BUT THE LOCALS ALWAYS HAVE TIME TO WELCOME A VISITOR AND ENJOY A GLASS OF SWEET TURKISH TEA!

WHERE NEXT?

LET'S TAKE A QUICK FLIGHT TO OUR NEXT CITY, BUT HOW QUICK WILL IT BE? YOU CHOOSE...

FLY 1 HR 20 MINS

GO TO **P68**

FLY 2 HRS 50 MINS

GO TO **P150**

THE TÜNEL

ONE OF THE BEST WAYS TO GET AROUND ISTANBUL AND AVOID THE CROWDS IS BY UNDERGROUND FUNICULAR. THERE ARE ONLY TWO LINES, TRAVELING BETWEEN TWO STATIONS, SO WE SHOULDN'T GET LOST! THE TÜNEL, WHICH OPENED IN 1875, IS THE WORLD'S SECOND-OLDEST WORKING UNDERGROUND LINE – ONLY THE LONDON TUBE IS OLDER.

QUEENSLAND

WELCOME TO CAIRNS! WE'RE IN QUEENSLAND, AUSTRALIA, ALSO KNOWN AS "THE SUNSHINE STATE." LET'S GO FOR A REFRESHING DIP, AND WHERE BETTER THAN THE GREAT BARRIER REEF – A HUGE UNDERWATER ECOSYSTEM THAT STRETCHES FOR 1,800 MI (3,000 KM) ALONG QUEENSLAND'S COAST. WITH WATER AS WARM AS A BATH, IT IS THE IDEAL PLACE TO SNORKEL AND LOOK FOR OVER 1,500 NATIVE FISH SPECIES AND 30 VARIETIES OF DOLPHIN THAT LIVE HERE.

UH OH! YOU ARE SO DISTRACTED BY THIS INCREDIBLE UNDERWATER WORLD THAT YOU MISS YOUR BOAT BACK TO SHORE AND WIND UP MAROONED ON AN ISLAND! YOU'LL HAVE TO WAIT TO BE RESCUED. THEN IT'S BACK TO THE BEGINNING FOR YOU.

DEAD END!

THERE ARE MORE THAN 900 ISLANDS IN THE GREAT BARRIER REEF.

MANILA!

HERE WE ARE IN THE CAPITAL OF THE PHILIPPINES – A MODERN MEGA–CITY THAT CAN BE CRAZY AND CHAOTIC ONE MINUTE AND COOL AND CHARMING THE NEXT. LET'S CHECK OUT THE AMAZING CITY HALL, WHICH IS SHAPED LIKE THE SHIELD OF A MEDIEVAL KNIGHT. THEN WE'LL EXPLORE SOME OF THE SECRET PASSAGEWAYS BENEATH THE CITY!

THE MARIKINA SHOE MUSEUM IS HOME TO THE WORLD'S LARGEST PAIR OF SHOES! THEY MEASURE MORE THAN 16 FT (5 M) LONG AND 7.9 FT (2.4 M) WIDE!

CLIMB ABOARD A JEEPNEY

THE MOST FUN WAY TO TRAVEL AROUND THE CITY IS IN A JEEPNEY. YOU CAN'T MISS THESE OLD JEEPS PAINTED IN EVERY COLOR OF THE RAINBOW AND CRAMMED WITH PASSENGERS. THEY DON'T STOP FOR LONG THOUGH, SO BE PREPARED TO JUMP ON AND OFF AS THEY SLOW DOWN!

WHERE NEXT?

DO WE HAVE ENOUGH PESOS TO PAY FOR A TAXI TO THE AIRPORT? IT'S TIME TO GO.

FLY 3 HRS
GO TO P64

FLY 15 HRS
GO TO P150

TIME TO MARVEL AT...

MONTREAL!

LET'S CHECK OUT CANADA'S SECOND-BIGGEST CITY. IN THE PROVINCE OF QUEBEC, IT'S A GREAT PLACE TO PRACTICE FRENCH – THE NUMBER-ONE LANGUAGE HERE. THIS CULTURAL HOT SPOT HAS AMAZING SHOWS, EXHIBITIONS, AND FESTIVALS ALL YEAR ROUND. BELOWGROUND, THERE ARE MILES OF TUNNELS FULL OF SHOPS AND MUSEUMS, SO LET'S GO!

MONTREAL IS NAMED AFTER MOUNT ROYAL HILL, OR *MONT ROYAL* IN FRENCH. NO BUILDING IN THE CITY IS ALLOWED TO BE TALLER THAN THE CROSS AT THE TOP OF THE HILL.

WHERE NEXT?

HAD YOUR FILL OF MONTREAL? TIME TO HOP ON THE NEXT FLIGHT OUT OF HERE!

FLY 6 HRS

GO TO P126

FLY 1 HR 15 MINS

GO TO P112

DINNERTIME

MAKE SURE YOU TRY POUTINE WHILE YOU'RE HERE, MONTREAL'S FAMOUS DISH OF FRENCH FRIES AND CHEESE CURDS COVERED IN GRAVY. IF YOU HAVE A SWEET TOOTH, THEN GO TO A SUGAR SHACK AND TASTE MAPLE SYRUP ON PANCAKES. MOST OF THE WORLD'S MAPLE SYRUP IS MADE HERE IN QUEBEC.

RIDE A CAMEL IN...
MARRAKECH!

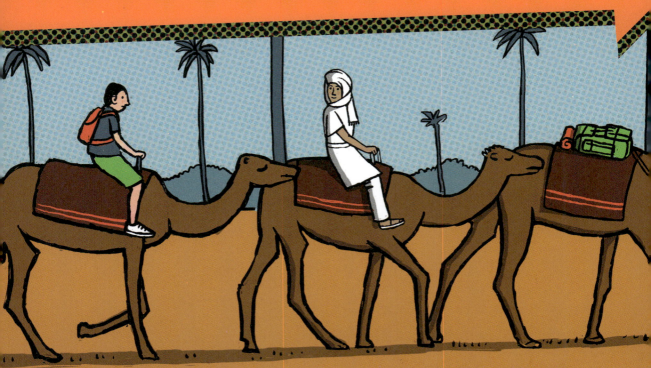

MARRAKECH IS A CITY IN MOROCCO WITH A SURPRISE AROUND EVERY CORNER. LET'S TAKE A CAMEL RIDE THROUGH PALMERAIE, A HUGE FOREST OF PALM TREES NORTH OF THE CITY. A JOURNEY ON ONE OF THESE SWAYING "SHIPS OF THE DESERT" FOLLOWED BY A CUP OF FRESH MINT TEA IS THE PERFECT WAY TO RELAX IN THE HEAT! THEN WE'LL MAKE OUR WAY TO DJEMAA EL FNA – THE CENTRAL SQUARE – WHICH AT NIGHT COMES ALIVE WITH DANCERS, STORYTELLERS, AND SNAKE CHARMERS!

CAMELS HAVE TWO ROWS OF THICK EYELASHES THAT HELP PROTECT THEIR EYES FROM DESERT DUST.

WHERE NEXT?

MOROCCO WILL BE A HARD ACT TO FOLLOW, BUT IT'S TIME TO LEAVE NORTH AFRICA.

FLY 7 HRS

GO TO **P134**

FLY 5 HRS 30 MINS

GO TO **P42**

VISIT THE SOUKS

MARRAKECH HAS A GREAT MAZE OF SOUKS (OPEN-AIR MARKETS), AND IT'S EASY TO GET LOST, SO STAY CLOSE. JAM-PACKED WITH STALLS, IT'S THE PERFECT PLACE TO BAG YOURSELF A BARGAIN, BUT BE PREPARED TO HAGGLE HARD TO GET A GOOD PRICE!

SCOUT OUT...

KOLKATA!

THE SUNDARBANS

A SHORT TRIP OUT OF THE CITY TAKES US TO THE SUNDARBANS NATIONAL PARK. INDIA AND BANGLADESH SHARE THIS COASTAL FOREST, HOME TO SALTWATER CROCODILES, GANGES RIVER DOLPHINS, AND ROYAL BENGAL TIGERS.

KOLKATA, OR CALCUTTA AS IT WAS KNOWN UNTIL 2001, IS THE SECOND–LARGEST CITY IN INDIA AND LIES IN WEST BENGAL PROVINCE. BUILT ON THE BANK OF THE HOOGHLY RIVER, THE CITY IS A JUMBLE OF CRUMBLING OLD BUILDINGS, GREAT MODERN SKYSCRAPERS, AND RAMBLING SHANTYTOWNS.

WHERE NEXT?

KOLKATA WAS A LITTLE CRAZY, BUT TOTALLY UNFORGETTABLE.

FLY 3 HRS
GO TO P56

FLY 4 HRS
GO TO P116

STREET LIFE

WANDER THE CITY'S BACKSTREETS, AND YOU'LL DISCOVER ASTONISHING SIGHTS, SOUNDS, AND SMELLS. WHETHER IT'S A BUSTLING NIGHT MARKET, HAWKERS OFFERING YOU CUPS OF CHAI TEA, OR A COW WANDERING DOWN THE ROAD, KOLKATA MAY NOT BE A PLACE TO RELAX, BUT YOU'LL NEVER FORGET ITS INCREDIBLE SPIRIT.

LET'S HULA IN...

HONOLULU!

SAY ALOHA TO HONOLULU, CAPITAL OF THE PACIFIC OCEAN PARADISE THAT IS HAWAII. WELCOME TO A BIG CITY FULL OF HISTORY – THERE'S NOWHERE TO BEAT IT IF YOU LIKE BEACH LIFE. THE WAVES ARE SO BIG HERE THAT IT'S ONE OF THE BEST PLACES ON EARTH TO GO SURFING – JUST MAKE SURE YOU DON'T WIPE OUT!

WELCOME TO WAIKIKI

WE'LL HEAD FOR WAIKIKI, THE CITY'S MOST FAMOUS BEACH – EVER SINCE THE HAWAIIAN ROYAL FAMILY CAME HERE TO RIDE ITS WAVES IN THE 1800S. IF YOU'D RATHER STAY ON DRY LAND, WE COULD TRY DOING THE HULA – HAWAII'S TRADITIONAL DANCE. SLIP A GARLAND OF FLOWERS AROUND YOUR NECK AND SWAY YOUR HIPS TO THE HULA BEAT!

IN HONOLULU, YOU CAN BE ARRESTED FOR ANNOYING A BIRD IN A PARK!

WHERE NEXT?

A PLACE THIS LAID-BACK IS HARD TO LEAVE, BUT IT'S TIME TO GO.

FLY 5 HRS
GO TO P126

FLY 10 HRS
GO TO P102

COME SEE THE SIGHTS OF...

MUMBAI!

MUMBAI, THE BIGGEST CITY IN INDIA, IS HOME TO 18 MILLION PEOPLE! AS WE WALK AROUND ITS ANCIENT STREETS, BREATHING IN THE AROMA OF SPICY STREET FOOD, LET'S COOL DOWN WITH A LASSI – A YOGURT-LIKE DRINK POPULAR WITH THE LOCALS. WHY NOT THEN SPEND A FEW RUPEES AT CHOR BAZAAR, THE CITY'S GIANT FLEA MARKET?

BEEP BEEP!

A GREAT WAY TO GET AROUND TOWN IS IN ONE OF MUMBAI'S 250,000 BLACK-AND-YELLOW AUTO RICKSHAWS. RIDING ALONG IN THESE THREE-WHEELER VEHICLES IS ALWAYS AN ADVENTURE. HEY, LET'S CATCH A RIDE TO THE MOVIE THEATER TO WATCH ONE OF THE SPECTACULAR BOLLYWOOD MOVIES PRODUCED IN THE CITY.

WHERE NEXT?

SAY GOODBYE TO ALL THE PEOPLE WE'VE MET, OR "MUMBAIKARS" AS THEY'RE CALLED HERE.

FLY 2 HRS

GO TO P116

FLY 6 HRS

GO TO P86

MEET THE AMAZING STONE PEOPLE OF...

EASTER ISLAND!

WE'VE ARRIVED ON EASTER ISLAND, A REMOTE PLACE IN THE MIDDLE OF THE PACIFIC OCEAN. THERE ARE NEARLY 900 INCREDIBLE STATUES OF HUMAN STONE FIGURES AROUND THE ISLAND. THEY WERE CARVED CENTURIES AGO BY THE RAPA NUI PEOPLE WHO HAVE LIVED HERE FOR OVER A THOUSAND YEARS.

ISLAND PARADISE

EASTER ISLAND REALLY IS A PLACE WHERE YOU CAN GET AWAY FROM IT ALL – THE NEAREST INHABITED ISLAND IS OVER 1,200 MI (2,000 KM) AWAY. ONCE WE'VE SEEN THE MYSTERIOUS STATUES – WHOSE BODIES ARE BURIED BELOWGROUND – WE'LL GO SNORKELING OFF THE PERFECT WHITE BEACHES.

WHERE NEXT?

FLY SIX HOURS BACK TO SANTIAGO IN CHILE, THEN GET A CONNECTING FLIGHT.

FLY 15 HRS
GO TO **P70**

FLY 2 HRS
GO TO **P106**

JACOB ROGGEVEEN, A DUTCH EXPLORER AND THE FIRST EUROPEAN TO LAND HERE, ARRIVED ON EASTER SUNDAY, 1722 WHICH IS HOW THE ISLAND GOT ITS NAME.

HAVE A BALL IN...

HAVANA!

HAVANA, OR *LA HABANA* AS IT IS KNOWN TO LOCALS, IS THE VIBRANT CAPITAL CITY OF CUBA, AN ISLAND IN THE CARIBBEAN. ALTHOUGH THIS COUNTRY LIES ONLY 100 MI (160 KM) FROM FLORIDA, IT FEELS LIKE ANOTHER WORLD! MANY OF HAVANA'S BUILDINGS LOOK OLD AND UNLOVED, BUT THIS IS A TOWN BURSTING WITH LIFE – LISTEN FOR CUBA'S MUSICAL MIX OF SPANISH GUITARS, SALSA, AND AFRO-CARIBBEAN RHYTHMS.

WHERE NEXT?

TIME TO LEAVE THOSE CUBAN BEATS BEHIND AND HOP ON A PLANE TO...

FLY 4 HRS
GO TO P146

FLY 2 HRS 45 MINS
GO TO P26

THE MALECÓN

ONE OF THE BEST PLACES TO GET A FEEL OF THE REAL HAVANA IS THE MALECÓN – AN OCEAN ROAD THAT RUNS FOR MILES. WE'LL WATCH AS THE WAVES CRASH OVER THE SEAWALL AND LOOK FOR THE CROWDS OF PEOPLE WHO COME HERE EVERY NIGHT TO SING, DANCE, AND TALK ABOUT THE EVENTS OF THE DAY.

BRUSSELS!

BRUSSELS, CAPITAL OF BELGIUM, IS A REAL MIX OF A CITY. IT'S BEEN AN IMPORTANT TOWN FOR OVER A THOUSAND YEARS, SO PARTS OF THE CITY ARE VERY OLD. BUT AS THE UNOFFICIAL CAPITAL OF THE EUROPEAN UNION, IT HAS PLENTY OF HIP, MODERN BUILDINGS, TOO.

CAFÉ LIFE

THE BEST WAY TO TAKE IT ALL IN IS FROM ONE OF THE CAFÉS ON THE CITY'S BEAUTIFUL MAIN SQUARE. LET'S TRY SOME DELICIOUS BELGIAN CHOCOLATE. THEN WE'LL VISIT A FAMOUS LANDMARK – A SMALL STATUE OF A BOY HAVING A PEE! ON MOST DAYS, YOU'LL FIND HIM DRESSED IN ONE OF THE 700 COSTUMES SPECIALLY MADE FOR HIM.

WHERE NEXT?

HOLD ON TO YOUR EUROS, YOU MAY NEED THEM AGAIN.

FLY 3 HRS 30 MINS

GO TO P154

FLY 2 HRS

GO TO P100

HANOI!

HANOI, THE CAPITAL OF VIETNAM, HAS BEEN THE COUNTRY'S MOST IMPORTANT CITY FOR OVER A THOUSAND YEARS. IN THE EARLY 20TH CENTURY, IT WAS RULED BY THE FRENCH, WHICH EXPLAINS WHY IT IS SOMETIMES CALLED "THE PARIS OF THE EAST." LET'S ESCAPE THE BUSY STREETS FULL OF WHIZZING MOPEDS, AND HEAD TO THE SHORES OF HOAN KIEM LAKE FOR SOME GENTLE EARLY-MORNING EXERCISE CALLED TAI CHI.

CYCLO POWER

WANT TO TAKE A CYCLO AROUND THE OLD QUARTER OR CHECK OUT THE LAKE? A CYCLO IS A THREE-WHEELED BICYCLE THAT LOCALS USE AS A TAXI. IT'S A BIT OF A TIGHT SQUEEZE, BUT THERE SHOULD BE ROOM FOR THE TWO OF US. KEEP AN EYE OUT FOR SOME UNUSUAL LOADS. YOU MIGHT SEE A CYCLO CARRYING HEAVY FURNITURE AND EVEN FARM ANIMALS!

SNAIL NOODLE SOUP IS ONE OF HANOI'S SPECIALTY DISHES. IT'S SLURPY AND SLIMY!

WHERE NEXT?

NOI BAI AIRPORT IS ONLY A SHORT BUS RIDE AWAY, THEN WE'RE OFF...

FLY 1 HR

GO TO P76

FLY 21 HRS

GO TO P30

YOU MADE IT!

CONGRATULATIONS! YOU'VE MADE IT ALL THE WAY BACK TO WHERE WE STARTED. LONDON!

BEFORE WE HAVE A WELL-EARNED REST, JOIN ME FOR ONE LAST TRIP – A NIGHTTIME FLIGHT ON THE LONDON EYE, AS WE SOAR INTO THE SKY AND LOOK DOWN ON THE CITY SPREAD OUT BENEATH US. WHY DON'T WE PLAN OUR NEXT ADVENTURE?

WHAT AN ADVENTURE IT'S BEEN! WE'VE EXPLORED INCREDIBLE DESTINATIONS ON EACH OF THE WORLD'S CONTINENTS AND TRIED OUT THE MOST EXCITING WAYS OF GETTING FROM ONE PLACE TO ANOTHER. WE'VE DODGED DISASTERS, DUCKED DEAD-ENDS, AND STAYED ON COURSE ALL THE WAY. IT TRULY HAS BEEN THE TRIP OF A LIFETIME, AND YOU HAVE BEEN THE BEST TRAVELING COMPANION. READY TO GO AGAIN?

EXPLORE ANCIENT...

ATHENS!

LET'S DISCOVER ONE OF THE WORLD'S OLDEST AND MOST FASCINATING CITIES. ATHENS, THE CAPITAL OF GREECE, WAS ONCE THE MOST IMPORTANT CITY IN THE ANCIENT WORLD. THE HOME OF GREAT ARTISTS, WRITERS, AND PHILOSOPHERS, ATHENS ALSO GAVE US IMPORTANT IDEAS SUCH AS DEMOCRACY, WHICH SAYS THAT EVERYONE SHOULD HAVE AN EQUAL SAY IN WHO GOVERNS THEM.

THE PARTHENON

OUR VISIT WOULDN'T BE COMPLETE WITHOUT
A VISIT TO THE ACROPOLIS, THE ANCIENT
FORTRESS ON TOP OF A ROCKY HILL OVERLOOKING
THE CITY. WE'LL SEE THE PARTHENON THERE – A
TEMPLE BUILT 2,500 YEARS AGO TO HONOR THE
GODDESS ATHENA. IT WAS THE MOST IMPORTANT
BUILDING IN ANCIENT GREECE.

WHERE NEXT?

THE SUN IS SHINING, AND
THE SEA IS BLUE, BUT
THERE'S NO TIME FOR
SWIMMING!

FLY 3 HRS 30 MINS
GO TO P108

FLY 10 HRS
GO TO P88

ATHENS HOSTED THE FIRST OLYMPIC GAMES IN 776 BC,
AS WELL AS THE FIRST MODERN OLYMPICS, IN 1896.

LIVE IT UP IN...

BARCELONA!

EXPLORING BARCELONA IS A REAL ADVENTURE! WE'RE IN SPAIN'S SECOND-BIGGEST CITY AFTER MADRID, AND THE CAPITAL OF THE CATALONIA REGION. IT'S ALL HERE – AMAZING MUSEUMS AND BEAUTIFUL GALLERIES, FANTASTIC SHOPS AND TAPAS BARS, STREET ENTERTAINERS AND SANDY BEACHES! IF WE'RE LUCKY ENOUGH TO GET A TICKET, A TRIP TO SEE BARCELONA'S WORLD-CLASS SOCCER TEAM IS A DREAM COME TRUE FOR ANY SOCCER FAN.

ANTONI GAUDÍ

ON OUR WAY THROUGH THE CITY, WE'LL SEE LOTS OF BEAUTIFUL, CRAZY BUILDINGS THAT ALMOST SEEM TO WOBBLE. THESE ARE THE WORK OF THE ARCHITECT ANTONI GAUDÍ, WHO DESIGNED BUILDINGS LIKE NO ONE ELSE. HIS MOST FAMOUS BUILDING IS THE SAGRADA FAMILIA CHURCH – WORK ON IT STARTED IN 1882 BUT IT'S STILL NOT FINISHED!

WHERE NEXT?

GOODBYE BARCELONA!
OR, *ADIOS*, AS THEY SAY
IN SPANISH.

FLY 2 HRS 30 MINS
GO TO P108

FLY 10 HRS
GO TO P56

THE NOU CAMP
STADIUM WHERE
THE BARCELONA
SOCCER TEAM
PLAYS IS EUROPE'S
LARGEST, WITH
ROOM FOR 99,000
SPECTATORS!

TRONDHEIM!

BACK IN THE 11TH CENTURY, WHEN VIKINGS RULED NORWAY, TRONDHEIM USED TO BE THE CAPITAL CITY. IN THOSE DAYS, IT WAS CALLED NIDAROS. TODAY, TRONDHEIM IS A LAID-BACK CITY FULL OF COOL CAFÉS AND GREAT MUSIC VENUES. IT'S THE PERFECT SIZE TO GET AROUND IN A DAY, SO LET'S HEAD FOR THE BAKKLANDET AREA IN THE CITY CENTER – IT'S HISTORIC AND PRETTY AND A GREAT PLACE FOR A BICYCLE RIDE.

THE NIDAROS CATHEDRAL IN TRONDHEIM IS WHERE THE KINGS OF NORWAY WERE CROWNED.

WHERE NEXT?

SPEND YOUR LAST FEW KRONER ON SOME TASTY SMOKED SALMON BEFORE YOU...

FLY 2 HRS 30 MINS

GO TO **P14**

FLY 3 HRS 15 MINS

GO TO **P22**

THE TRAMPE

FOR AN EXTRA BIT OF EXCITEMENT, WE'LL TAKE THE TRAMPE – THE WORLD'S ONLY BICYCLE ESCALATOR! KEEP ONE FOOT ON THE PEDAL AND PUT THE OTHER ON THE FOOTPLATE. THEN LET THE TRAMPE DRAG YOU UP BRUBAKKEN HILL. DON'T WORRY – YOU'LL GET THE HANG OF IT!

JUMP INTO A...

JUMBO JET

THE JUMBO JET IS THE NICKNAME FOR THE BOEING 747, WHICH WAS THE WORLD'S FIRST DOUBLE-DECKER PASSENGER AIRPLANE. IT FIRST FLEW IN 1970 AND SOON BECAME THE MOST POPULAR AIRPLANE FOR TOURISTS JETTING ACROSS THE GLOBE. I'VE GOT US SEATS ON THE TOP DECK, WHERE WE'LL BE ABLE TO SIT BACK, RELAX, AND ENJOY AN IN-FLIGHT MOVIE.

IN THE COCKPIT

IT TAKES A LOT OF SKILL TO FLY ONE OF THESE METAL BEASTS. IN THE COCKPIT, THE PILOT IS IN CHARGE OF A CONTROL PANEL WITH 365 SWITCHES, DIALS, AND LIGHTS. INCREDIBLY, 747S HAVE CARRIED OVER 3.5 BILLION PASSENGERS – THAT'S EQUAL TO HALF OF THE WORLD'S ENTIRE POPULATION!

NASA (NORTH AMERICAN SPACE AGENCY) USED JUMBO JETS TO TRANSPORT THEIR SPACE SHUTTLES BEFORE THEY BLASTED OFF INTO SPACE.

FLY 5 HRS
GO TO P156

FLY 17 HRS
GO TO P140

FLY 11 HRS
GO TO P130

WHERE NEXT?

THIS ONE'S A LONG HAUL, BUT ON WHICH CONTINENT WILL YOU LAND?

LUANG PRABANG!

LUANG PRABANG IS A CITY IN THE ASIAN KINGDOM OF LAOS WHERE TIME SEEMS TO HAVE STOOD STILL. IT SITS WHERE TWO GREAT RIVERS MEET – THE NAM KHAN AND THE MEKONG – AND IS FULL OF TEMPLES AND MONASTERIES, NOT TO MENTION BEAUTIFUL WATERFALLS. IT'S THE PERFECT PLACE TO COME FOR PEACE AND QUIET.

ONE OF THE MOST POPULAR SPORTS IN LAOS IS KATOR, WHICH IS LIKE VOLLEYBALL EXCEPT THAT PLAYERS USE THEIR FEET INSTEAD OF THEIR HANDS.

WHERE NEXT?

A QUICK RIDE IN A TUK-TUK WILL TAKE US AWAY FROM THIS BEAUTIFUL CITY TO THE AIRPORT.

FLY 2 HRS DRIVE 3 HRS

GO TO **P138**

GO TO P138

FLY 3 HRS 15 MINS

GO TO **P120**

GO TO P120

THE PAK OU CAVES

I'M GOING TO TAKE YOU OUT OF THE CITY FOR A COOL TRIP TO THE NEARBY PAK OU CAVES. THEY LIE DEEP INSIDE A MOUNTAIN, AND MONKS USED TO LIVE HERE. AS WE WANDER THROUGH, LET'S SEE HOW MANY STATUES OF BUDDHA WE CAN COUNT – THERE ARE THOUSANDS LINING THE PASSAGES!

TIME TO RIDE THE...
GREYHOUND BUS

GREYHOUND LINES IS PERHAPS THE MOST FAMOUS BUS COMPANY IN THE WORLD. BUY A TICKET AND NOT ONLY CAN YOU STOP OFF AT PRETTY MUCH ANY BIG TOWN IN THE US, BUT YOU CAN VISIT CANADA AND MEXICO, TOO. EACH YEAR, OVER 18 MILLION PASSENGERS MAKE USE OF THE 1,700 COACHES OWNED BY GREYHOUND – INCLUDING 400 RUNAWAY KIDS WHO GET A FREE RIDE HOME.

GREYHOUND BUSES TRAVEL TO 3,800 DIFFERENT DESTINATIONS!

WHERE NEXT?

WATCH THE WORLD ROLL BY AS YOU GAZE OUT OF THE WINDOW.

RIDE 68 HRS

GO TO P126

RIDE 8 HRS 30 MINS

GO TO P48

SPEEDY AS A...

THE GREYHOUND COMPANY WAS SET UP IN 1914 BY A SWEDE, CARL ERIC WICKMAN, WHO ORIGINALLY CAME TO AMERICA TO WORK AS A MINER. HOWEVER, IT WAS ANOTHER MEMBER OF THE FIRM WHO CAME UP WITH THE GREYHOUND NAME. WHEN HE SAW A REFLECTION OF ONE OF THE BUSES IN A WINDOW, IT REMINDED HIM OF THE FAMOUSLY SLEEK DOG

WISCONSIN!

WE'VE ARRIVED IN MILWAUKEE, THE LARGEST CITY IN THE US STATE OF WISCONSIN. IT SITS ON THE SHORELINE OF LAKE MICHIGAN, ONE OF THE FIVE GREAT LAKES THAT ARE SPREAD ACROSS THE US AND CANADA. WHETHER YOU LIKE TO GO OUT ON THE WATER OR PREFER HANGING AROUND ON DRY LAND, THERE IS ALWAYS PLENTY TO SEE AND DO ALONG THE WATERFRONT. AND WHEN WINTER HITS AND THE WEATHER IS REALLY BAD, WE CAN TAKE THE ICE ROAD!

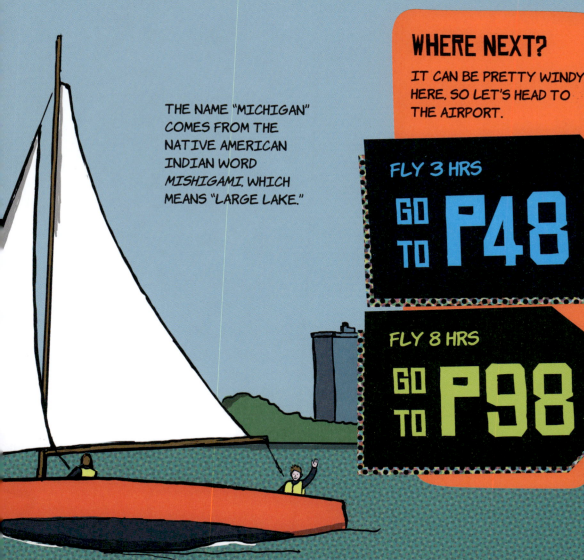

THE NAME "MICHIGAN" COMES FROM THE NATIVE AMERICAN INDIAN WORD *MISHIGAMI*, WHICH MEANS "LARGE LAKE."

WHERE NEXT?

IT CAN BE PRETTY WINDY HERE, SO LET'S HEAD TO THE AIRPORT.

FLY 3 HRS

GO TO P48

FLY 8 HRS

GO TO P98

THE ICE ROAD

I'VE ARRANGED A TRIP TO CHECK OUT THE ICE ANGEL THAT RUNS BETWEEN THE SMALL TOWN OF BAYFIELD AND NEARBY MADELINE ISLAND. FOR A FEW WEEKS EACH YEAR, THE WATER BETWEEN THESE TWO PLACES FREEZES OVER AND FORMS A TWO-MILE ICE HIGHWAY. THE ICE ANGEL IS AN ICE BOAT THAT SAILS ACROSS THE SURFACE LIKE A GIANT, JET-PROPELLED ICE SKATE!

TRY OUT HI-TECH...
TOKYO!

HELLO! OR KON'NICHIWA AND WELCOME TO TOKYO, CAPITAL OF JAPAN AND THE WORLD'S LARGEST CITY. THIS IS AN OLD CITY WITH A VERY MODERN FEEL. ONE MINUTE YOU'RE WANDERING AROUND ANCIENT TEMPLES AND THE NEXT YOU'RE WALKING DOWN A BRIGHT NEON-LIT STREET, WHERE GIANT SCREENS PLAY THE NEWEST POP VIDEOS TO COOL KIDS IN THE LATEST FASHION. THIS IS A CITY THAT LOVES TO KEEP UP-TO-DATE!

THE SKYTREE

TO GET THE BEST VIEWS OF THE CITY, I'M TAKING US FOR DINNER IN THE TOYKO SKYTREE. AT 2,080 FT (634 M), IT'S THE WORLD'S TALLEST TOWER. THEN IT'S BACK TO OUR CAPSULE HOTEL – A TOKYO SPECIALTY WHERE THE ROOMS ARE JUST A LITTLE BIGGER THAN A LARGE FRIDGE. IN A CITY THIS CRAMMED, NO ONE HAS TOO MUCH SPACE!

WHERE NEXT?

IT'S TIME TO QUIT THIS BUZZING METROPOLIS. SO, SHALL WE...

TAKE A TRAIN? GO TO P144

CATCH A PLANE? GO TO P30

A TIGHT SQUEEZE

THE TOKYO RAIL SYSTEM IS SO BUSY THAT THERE ARE "PUSHERS" WHOSE JOB IT IS TO SHOVE PASSENGERS ONTO CROWDED TRAINS.

東京

DUBAI!

WELCOME TO DUBAI, ONE OF SEVEN EMIRATES THAT MAKE UP THE UNITED ARAB EMIRATES IN THE MIDDLE EAST. WHEN OIL WAS DISCOVERED HERE HALF A CENTURY AGO, DUBAI QUICKLY BECAME SUPER-RICH. TODAY, IT IS ONE OF THE MOST POPULAR TOURIST DESTINATIONS IN THE WORLD, FAMOUS FOR ITS LUXURY HOTELS AND DESIGNER SHOPPING.

ARTIFICIAL ISLANDS

DUBAI'S COAST IS LIKE NO OTHER! THERE ARE FOUR MAN-MADE ISLANDS HERE, THE PALM ISLANDS AND THE WORLD ISLANDS – A MAP OF THE WORLD DRAWN ON WATER!

WHERE NEXT?

IT'S SO HOT HERE, SHALL WE LEAVE FOR SOMEWHERE COOLER?

FLY 3 HRS
GO TO **P36**

FLY 10 HRS
GO TO **P82**

FLY 14 HRS
GO TO **P118**

BEFORE YOU JET OFF, STOP IN AT THE DUBAI MALL TO VISIT CANDYLICIOUS – THE WORLD'S LARGEST CANDY SHOP.

THE BURJ KHALIFA

LET'S ZOOM UP THE WORLD'S TALLEST SKYSCRAPER, MEASURING A DIZZYING 2717 FT (828 M). YOU'LL FEEL LIKE YOU'RE FLYING AS THE ELEVATOR ZIPS UP 140 FLOORS AT 33 FT (10 M) PER SECOND. SPARE A THOUGHT FOR THE 36 WORKERS WHOSE JOB IT IS TO CLEAN THE TOWER'S 24,000 REFLECTIVE WINDOWS!

SIT BACK AND MARVEL AT...

MAURITIUS!

SO HERE WE ARE IN PORT LOUIS, THE CAPITAL CITY OF MAURITIUS – A BEAUTIFUL ISLAND NATION OFF THE EAST COAST OF AFRICA. LET'S GET UP EARLY AND WATCH THE SUN RISE OVER THE INDIAN OCEAN. THEN WE COULD TAKE A TRIP TO THE NATURAL HISTORY MUSEUM TO SEE THE SKELETON OF AN EXTINCT BIRD CALLED THE DODO. THIS FLIGHTLESS BIRD IS A SYMBOL OF MAURITIUS, SINCE THIS IS THE ONLY PLACE WHERE IT WAS KNOWN TO LIVE.

THE LAST DEFINITE SIGHTING OF A DODO WAS WAY BACK IN 1662

WHERE NEXT?

IT'S NOT EASY SAYING GOODBYE TO THIS ISLAND PARADISE.

FLY 2 HRS 30 MINS

GO TO P148

FLY 4 HRS 15 MINS

GO TO P32

FLIC-EN-FLAC BEACH

WE'RE OFF TO THE BEACH! THE REASON MOST TRAVELERS COME TO MAURITIUS IS TO ENJOY THE MANY GORGEOUS SEASIDE RESORTS. LET'S LAY DOWN OUR TOWELS ON THE WHITE SANDY BEACH AT FLIC-EN-FLAC AND SOAK UP SOME SUNSHINE. IF WE'RE REALLY LUCKY, WE MIGHT EVEN SEE ONE OF THE RARE PINK PIGEONS THAT LIVE HERE.

DELIGHT IN...
DHAKA!

DHAKA, THE CAPITAL OF BANGLADESH, IS A BIG, BUSTLING CITY THAT CAN FEEL A BIT OVERWHELMING AT FIRST. BUT IT'S NOT ALL CHAOTIC CROWDS AND BUSY ROADS. THE MIGHTY BURIGANGA RIVER IS AT THE HEART OF EVERYTHING THAT GOES ON HERE. THERE ARE BEAUTIFUL GREEN SPACES, TOO, AS WELL AS LOADS OF HISTORIC BUILDINGS. DHAKA HAS A FASCINATING PAST. IT'S BEEN PART OF THREE DIFFERENT COUNTRIES IN THE LAST 100 YEARS!

WHERE NEXT?

LET'S LEAVE THE HUSTLE AND BUSTLE OF DHAKA BEHIND FOR NOW.

FLY 4 HRS

GO TO P160

FLY 21 HRS

GO TO P156

DHAKA IS THE HOME OF CRICKET IN BANGLADESH AND IN THIS CITY PEOPLE PLAY IT EVERYWHERE – ON THE STREET, IN PARKS, ALLEYWAYS, AND EVEN ON ROOFTOPS!

BEAT THE CROWDS IN...
BANGKOK!

TODAY WE'RE IN THAILAND'S AWESOME AND EXCITING CAPITAL CITY. WE MIGHT BE CHATTING TO A MONK IN A BEAUTIFUL OLD TEMPLE ONE MOMENT, THEN HAGGLING FOR A BARGAIN IN THE HUGE CHATUCHAK MARKET. OR FEASTING ON YUMMY NOODLES ON A STREET CORNER AS THE PASSING CARS COVER US IN EXHAUST FUMES! THIS IS A CITY WITH MANY DIFFERENT SIDES!

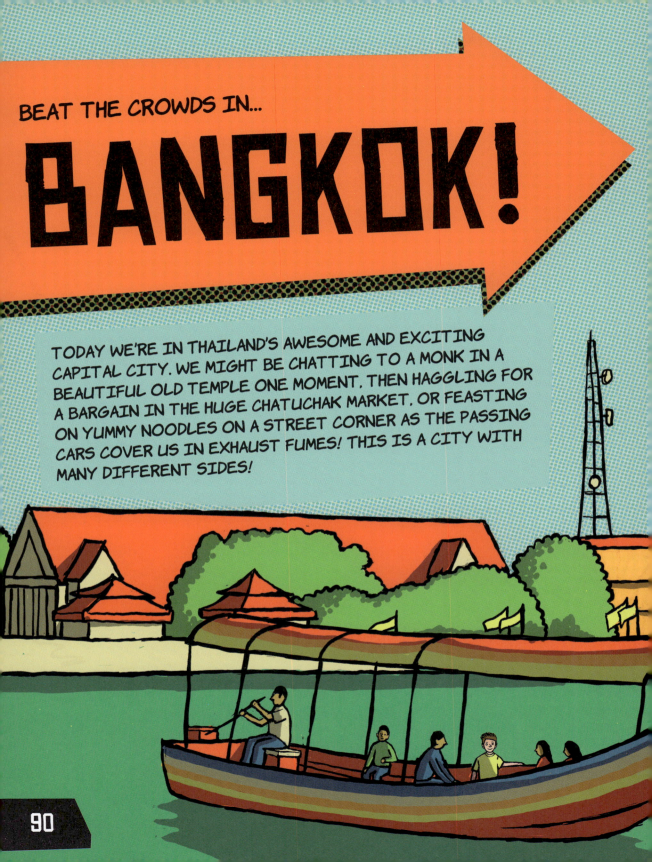

THE FULL NAME OF BANGKOK IN THAI IS A TONGUE-TWISTING 169 LETTERS LONG.

WHERE NEXT?

GOODBYE, OR LA-KON AS THEY SAY IN THAILAND.

CATCH A PLANE
GO TO P130

TAKE A BOAT
GO TO P152

RIVER TAXI

A GREAT WAY TO AVOID THE CROWDS IS TO BUY A TICKET FOR ONE OF THE CANAL TAXIS THAT TRAVEL UP AND DOWN THE SAEN SEAB CANAL, RIGHT THROUGH THE MIDDLE OF THE CITY. THERE ARE PLENTY OF THEM SO WE WON'T HAVE TO WAIT LONG, AND IT'S THE PERFECT WAY TO WATCH THE WORLD GO BY.

HIT THE ROAD IN A...

RENTAL CAR

WE'RE HEADING OFF ON THE ULTIMATE ROAD TRIP IN A GAS-GUZZLING RENTAL CAR. I'VE FILLED UP THE TANK AND CHECKED THE TIRES, SO WE'RE ALL SET FOR OUR NEXT ADVENTURE. PUT YOUR FAVORITE TUNES ON THE CAR STEREO AND GET READY TO COVER SOME SERIOUS MILEAGE.

IN 1984, SWISS COUPLE EMIL AND LILIANA SCHMID BEGAN THE LONGEST CAR JOURNEY IN HISTORY. THEY ARE STILL GOING, HAVING DRIVEN NEARLY 500,000 MI (805,000 KM) IN THE SAME VEHICLE!

AMERICAN DINER

WHY DON'T WE FIND A ROADSIDE DINER? THEN PARK OUTSIDE AND REFUEL INSIDE! WHAT WILL YOU HAVE? BACON AND EGGS AND A STACK OF PANCAKES? DEEP-FRIED CHICKEN OR SMOKY BARBECUED PORK? MAKE MINE A BURGER, FRIES, AND A SODA. THEN I'LL BE READY TO GET BEHIND THE WHEEL AGAIN!

31 HRS

GO TO **P102**

WHERE NEXT?

THAT ALL DEPENDS ON HOW LONG YOUR ROAD TRIP TAKES AND HOW MANY STOPS YOU MAKE...

20 HRS

GO TO **P124**

WE'VE ARRIVED IN ONE OF JAPAN'S PRETTIEST CITIES. WHILE OTHER PARTS OF THE COUNTRY LOVE TO BE CUTTING-EDGE AND MODERN, KYOTO IS A LITTLE MORE OLD-FASHIONED. IT'S SAID THAT THERE ARE 1,600 BUDDHIST TEMPLES HERE, SOME DATING BACK AS FAR AS THE YEAR 603. AS WELL AS ALL THE BEAUTIFUL, RELAXING GARDENS, WE'LL BE ABLE TO BUY TRADITIONAL JAPANESE FOOD LIKE TOFU, FISH, PICKLES, AND TEA.

UH OH! WHAT'S THAT THUNDERCLAP? WHERE IS EVERYONE GOING? OH DEAR, THE WEATHER FORECAST SAYS THERE'S A TYPHOON HEADING TOWARDS THE CITY. WE'D BETTER FIND SHELTER UNTIL IT'S OVER. I'M AFRAID THAT MEANS OUR JOURNEY HAS COME TO AN END. IT'S BACK TO THE START FOR YOU. BETTER LUCK NEXT TIME!

DEAD END!

KYOTO WAS THE CAPITAL OF IMPERIAL JAPAN FOR OVER 1,000 YEARS.

JOHANNESBL

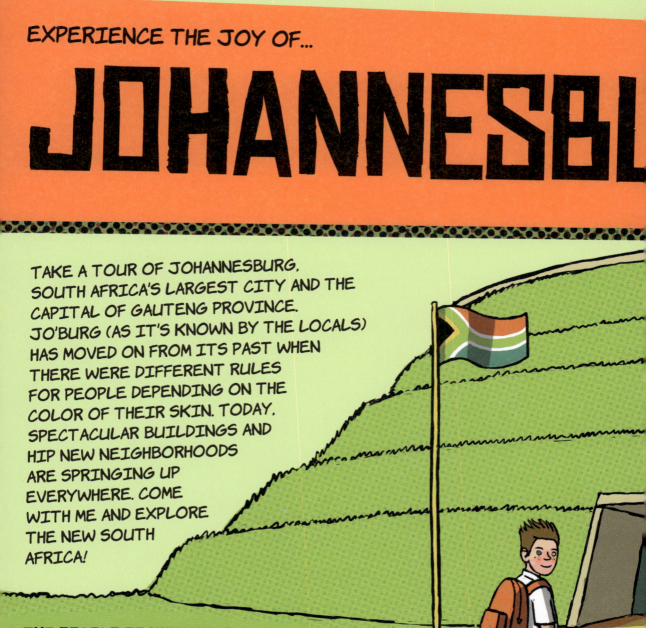

TAKE A TOUR OF JOHANNESBURG, SOUTH AFRICA'S LARGEST CITY AND THE CAPITAL OF GAUTENG PROVINCE. JO'BURG (AS IT'S KNOWN BY THE LOCALS) HAS MOVED ON FROM ITS PAST WHEN THERE WERE DIFFERENT RULES FOR PEOPLE DEPENDING ON THE COLOR OF THEIR SKIN. TODAY, SPECTACULAR BUILDINGS AND HIP NEW NEIGHBORHOODS ARE SPRINGING UP EVERYWHERE. COME WITH ME AND EXPLORE THE NEW SOUTH AFRICA!

THE CRADLE OF HUMANKIND

JUST AN HOUR FROM JO'BURG BY CAR AND WE'RE AT MAROPENG, AN AREA NICKNAMED "THE CRADLE OF CIVILIZATION."

RG!

ABOUT 40 PERCENT OF ALL THE GOLD EVER FOUND COMES FROM THE AREA AROUND JOHANNESBURG!

WHERE NEXT?

THERE'S SO MUCH TO SEE AND DO IN SOUTH AFRICA, BUT THE PLANE IS WAITING...

FLY 11 HRS 30 MINS

GO TO P30

FLY 15 HRS 30 MINS

GO TO P156

MAROPENG

OUR HUMAN ANCESTORS HAVE LIVED IN THIS PLACE FOR OVER 4 MILLION YEARS! SCIENTISTS HAVE FOUND LOADS OF AMAZING FOSSILS IN THE ANCIENT STERKFONTEIN CAVES – OVER 90,000 OF THEM – AND MORE THAN 9,000 STONE TOOLS USED BY EARLY HUMANS.

ALASKA!

WELCOME TO THE LARGEST STATE IN THE US. NOT MANY PEOPLE LIVE HERE, WHICH MEANS THERE'S A LOT OF SPACE TO ENJOY. IF YOU LIKE MOUNTAINS AND ICY WILDERNESS, THEN ALASKA IS THE PLACE FOR YOU. WE WON'T BE ENTIRELY ON OUR OWN THOUGH, BECAUSE IT'S TEEMING WITH WILDLIFE. JUST TRY NOT TO BUMP INTO A BROWN BEAR — THEY'RE HUGE AND NOT VERY CUDDLY!

WHERE NEXT?

WE'LL FLY OUT OF ANCHORAGE IN ALASKA. HOW LONG DO YOU WANT TO BE IN THE AIR?

FLY 6 HRS 30 MINS

GO TO P54

FLY 21 HRS

GO TO P36

TONGASS FOREST

WHEN YOU'VE SEEN ENOUGH MOUNTAINS AND ICY GLACIERS, WE CAN HEAD FOR TONGASS – THE BIGGEST NATIONAL FOREST IN THE US. THERE'S NO BETTER WAY TO EXPLORE THIS NATURAL WORLD THAN WHIZZING ALONG A ZIP WIRE, HIGH ABOVE THE TREETOPS. WHHHHEEEEEE!

THE UNITED STATES BOUGHT ALASKA FROM RUSSIA IN 1867 FOR JUST TWO CENTS PER ACRE. WHAT A BARGAIN!

EXPERIENCE THE BUZZ OF...

BUDAPEST!

BUDAPEST, THE CAPITAL OF HUNGARY, IS A REAL FEAST FOR THE EYES. THERE'S BEEN A CITY HERE ON THE BANKS OF THE RIVER DANUBE SINCE ROMAN TIMES. TODAY, THERE ARE MANY BEAUTIFUL BUILDINGS TO INVESTIGATE, EACH PLAYING A PART OF BUDAPEST'S LONG HISTORY. LET'S HEAD TO BUDA CASTLE, THEN TO HEROES' SQUARE AND ON TO THE PARLIAMENT BUILDING.

HOT CITY!

GETTING AROUND IS EASY, AS BUDAPEST HAS ONE OF THE OLDEST AND BEST TRAM SYSTEMS IN THE WORLD. AT THE END OF THE DAY, WE'LL COOL OFF IN ONE OF THE BATHHOUSES SPRINKLED AROUND THE CITY. BUDAPEST HAS MORE THERMAL SPRINGS THAN ANY OTHER CAPITAL CITY IN THE WORLD.

WHERE NEXT?

ALL THAT RELAXING HAS LEFT YOU REFRESHED AND READY FOR THE ROAD AGAIN...

CATCH A PLANE

GO TO P28

TAKE A BUS

GO TO P68

MAKE THE MOST OF...
MEXICO CITY

MEXICO CITY WAS ORIGINALLY BUILT ON A DRIED-OUT LAKE AND SINKS BY ABOUT 4 IN (10 CM) EVERY YEAR.

TEOTIHUACÁN

MEXICO CITY WAS ONCE THE MAIN CITY OF THE AZTEC PEOPLE, WHO CALLED IT TENOCHTITLAN. FOR A TASTE OF WHAT AZTEC LIFE MUST HAVE BEEN LIKE, I'VE ARRANGED A TRIP TO THE TEOTIHUACÁN ARCHAEOLOGICAL SITE TO SEE SOME AWESOME ANCIENT AZTEC PYRAMIDS.

IT'S IMPOSSIBLE TO GET BORED IN MEXICO CITY, THE LIVELY CAPITAL OF MEXICO. IT WAS AN IMPORTANT CITY LONG BEFORE THE SPANISH ARRIVED IN THE 16TH CENTURY, AND THERE ARE PLENTY OF MUSEUMS THAT TELL ITS INCREDIBLE STORY. BUT THIS IS A PLACE STILL WRITING ITS HISTORY, SO WE'LL MAKE TIME TO CHECK OUT ITS FAB ART AND MUSIC SCENES, AMAZING SPORTS, AND SENSATIONAL SPICY FOOD!

WHERE NEXT?

READY TO HEAD TO THE AIRPORT? HOW LONG WILL YOU STAY IN THE SKY?

MAKE A SHORT HOP

GO TO P60

TAKE A LONG TRIP

GO TO P74

MEXICAN WRESTLING

IT'S TIME TO GO BACK INTO TOWN FOR SOME MORE MODERN MEXICAN CULTURE — A BOUT OF CRAZILY ENTERTAINING MEXICAN WRESTLING!

WELLINGTON

ZEALANDIA

WELLINGTON HAS ALL THE THINGS YOU'D EXPECT IN A BIG CITY. THE MUSEUM OF NEW ZEALAND, TE PAPA TONGAREWA, FOR INSTANCE, TELLS THE HISTORY OF NEW ZEALAND, INCLUDING ITS NATIVE MAORI PEOPLE. BUT THIS IS A COUNTRY BEST ENJOYED OUTDOORS, SO LET'S HEAD FOR THE ZEALANDIA WILDLIFE RESERVE. HOPEFULLY, WE'LL SPOT A KIWI — A VERY SHY, FLIGHTLESS BIRD AND NEW ZEALAND'S NATIONAL SYMBOL.

WE'VE FOUND OUR WAY TO NEW ZEALAND – WELLINGTON TO BE PRECISE, THE WORLD'S MOST REMOTE AND SOUTHERLY CAPITAL CITY! IT'S A BEAUTY, TOO, BUILT ON THE SHORES OF NORTH ISLAND, ONE OF NEW ZEALAND'S TWO MAIN ISLANDS. WE'LL SEE THE AMAZING HARBOR, GOLDEN BEACHES, LUSH GREEN HILLSIDES, AND SNOWCAPPED MOUNTAINS. BRING A WARM COAT THOUGH – IT GETS WINDY HERE!

IN 1893 NEW ZEALAND BECAME THE FIRST COUNTRY TO GIVE WOMEN THE VOTE.

FLY 2 HRS, SAIL 2 WEEKS!
GO TO P24

WHERE NEXT?

YOU'RE SAD TO LEAVE THIS AMAZING COUNTRY, BUT YOU NEED TO PRESS ON.

FLY 4 HRS
GO TO P44

TANGO THROUGH...

BUENOS AIRE

LET ME SHOW YOU THE SIGHTS OF ARGENTINA'S CONFIDENT, BUZZING CAPITAL CITY. RULED BY SPAIN FOR CENTURIES, THIS IS A TOWN THAT LOOKS EUROPEAN BUT IS FULL OF SOUTH AMERICAN PASSION – AND NOT JUST FOR SOCCER. LIFE HERE IS LIVED ON THE STREETS, SO LET'S TAKE A STROLL AND TAKE IN THIS GEM OF A PLACE BEFORE WE TUCK INTO A HUGE ARGENTINE STEAK FOR DINNER.

IT TAKES TWO

AFTER DINNER, WHAT BETTER WAY TO WORK OFF THE CALORIES THAN WITH DANCING? LEGEND HAS IT THAT THE ROMANTIC ARGENTINE TANGO WAS INVENTED IN THE BACKSTREETS OF BUENOS AIRES WAY BACK IN THE 19TH CENTURY. TODAY, THERE IS NO SHORTAGE OF PLACES TO WATCH PROFESSIONALS STRUT THEIR STUFF, OR EVEN HAVE A GO YOURSELF!

THERE ARE NO LESS THAN 24 PROFESSIONAL CLUBS IN THIS SOCCER-CRAZY CITY.

S!

WHERE NEXT?

WAVE GOODBYE TO THE PORTEÑOS – THE PEOPLE OF BUENOS AIRES.

TAKE A BOAT

GO TO P24

CATCH A PLANE

GO TO P126

AMSTERDAM!

MUSEUM CENTRAL

I WANT TO TAKE YOU TO TWO GREAT MUSEUMS. THE FIRST HOUSES PAINTINGS BY ONE OF THE NETHERLANDS' MOST FAMOUS ARTISTS, VINCENT VAN GOGH. PERHAPS YOU'VE SEEN HIS PAINTINGS OF SUNFLOWERS? THEN IT'S OVER TO ANNE FRANK'S HOUSE, WHERE WE'LL LEARN ALL ABOUT THE BRAVE YOUNG GIRL WHO KEPT A DIARY OF HER LIFE IN THE CITY DURING THE SECOND WORLD WAR.

I CAN'T WAIT TO SHOW YOU AMSTERDAM, CAPITAL OF THE NETHERLANDS. THE CITY BEGAN LIFE AS A SMALL FISHING VILLAGE IN THE 12TH CENTURY AND GOT ITS NAME FROM THE RIVER AMSTEL THAT FLOWS THROUGH ITS HEART. THESE DAYS AMSTERDAM IS A VERY COOL, FUN CITY. LET'S HOP ON OUR BIKES LIKE THE LOCALS AND EXPLORE! THEN TAKE A BOAT ON ONE OF THE CITY'S 165 CANALS.

EVERY YEAR, 25,000 BIKES END UP IN THE CITY'S CANALS. BE CAREFUL HOW YOU RIDE!

FLY SHORT-HAUL
GO TO **P14**

FLY LONG-HAUL
GO TO **P60**

ON YOUR BIKE
GO TO **P132**

WHERE NEXT?

DO YOU TAKE TO THE ROAD OR MAKE YOUR WAY TO SCHIPHOL AIRPORT?

YOU'RE ON A
EUROPEAN CRUISE

AFTER CRUISING ACROSS THE ATLANTIC, YOU'VE SWAPPED THE WIDE OPEN SEA FOR THE RHINE, ELBE, AND DANUBE – JUST A FEW OF THE MANY MAGNIFICENT RIVERS THAT WIND THEIR WAY FOR THOUSANDS OF MILES THROUGH THE COUNTRIES OF EUROPE. SITTING ON THE DECK OF A RIVER CRUISER IS A GREAT WAY TO GET A FLAVOR OF THE DIFFERENT LANDSCAPES AND CULTURES THAT MAKE UP MODERN EUROPE, SO LET'S RELAX AND ENJOY THE VIEWS.

A WORLD OF SITES

BIG CITIES AND TINY VILLAGES, BEAUTIFUL FORESTS, STUNNING MOUNTAINS — EUROPE HAS IT ALL, AND MUCH MORE, TOO. YOU'LL SAIL FROM THE TULIP FIELDS OF HOLLAND PAST ELEGANT FRENCH CHATEAUX, TOWERING GERMAN CASTLES, AND THE ANCIENT CITIES OF BUDAPEST, AND, FINALLY, PRAGUE.

WHERE NEXT?

PRAGUE'S OUR FINAL RIVER STOP. LET'S TAKE TO THE AIR AGAIN.

FLY 2 HRS 25 MINS

GO TO P70

FLY 1 HR 30 MINS

GO TO P38

EUROPE IS MADE UP OF ABOUT 50 NATIONS, INCLUDING THE WORLD'S SMALLEST COUNTRY — THE VATICAN

DISCOVER... TORONTO!

TORONTO IS THE LARGEST CITY IN CANADA AND CAPITAL OF THE PROVINCE OF ONTARIO. IT'S A TRUE 21ST-CENTURY SUPER-CITY, WHERE DIFFERENT CULTURES MEET. HALF THE POPULATION COMES FROM COUNTRIES OTHER THAN CANADA! ABOUT 140 LANGUAGES ARE SPOKEN, WHICH MAKES THIS CITY ONE OF THE MOST COSMOPOLITAN ANYWHERE.

HOCKEY HALL OF FAME

THERE IS LOADS TO SEE AND DO HERE — FAB MUSEUMS, GREAT THEATER, A WORLD-CLASS ZOO, NOT TO MENTION THE CN TOWER AND ITS UNBEATABLE VIEWS. BUT FOR A TASTE OF WHAT MAKES TORONTO TICK, I RECOMMEND A VISIT TO THE HOCKEY HALL OF FAME. WE'LL FIND OUT WHY CANADIANS ARE CRAZY ABOUT ICE HOCKEY, ESPECIALLY THE LOCAL HEROES WHO PLAY FOR THE TORONTO MAPLE LEAFS.

TORONTO HAS A NETWORK OF UNDERGROUND PEDESTRIAN PATHS THAT STRETCHES FOR 17 MI (28 KM).

WHERE NEXT?

IT'S A SHAME TO LEAVE THIS GREAT CITY, BUT TIME TO GO TO PEARSON AIRPORT.

FLY 15 HRS 30 MINS

GO TO P32

FLY 10 HRS

GO TO P42

NORTH POLE

YOU'RE ON TOP OF THE WORLD!

YOU'VE ARRIVED AT THE NORTH POLE – THE NORTHERNMOST POINT ON THE PLANET AND THE ONLY PLACE ON EARTH WHERE EVERY WAY YOU TURN IS SOUTH! LET'S TAKE TO THE SKIES IN A HOT–AIR BALLOON. FROM 130 FT (40 M) UP, WE CAN SURVEY THE VAST ICY WILDERNESS THAT SEEMS TO STRETCH ON FOREVER.

ICE SAFARI

BECAUSE THE WINDS AT THE NORTH POLE CAN BE VERY STRONG, OUR BALLOON IS SECURELY TIED TO AN ICEBREAKER – A SPECIAL KIND OF SHIP BUILT TO SAIL THROUGH ICE-COVERED WATERS. KEEP YOUR EYES PEELED FOR THE NATIVE WILDLIFE – IF YOU'RE LUCKY. YOU MAY SPY A POLAR BEAR. A RINGED SEAL. OR EVEN A WHALE.

FEBRUARY IS THE COLDEST MONTH TO VISIT THE NORTH POLE. TEMPERATURES HAVE BEEN KNOWN TO DROP TO A BONE-CHILLING -58°F (-50°C)

WHERE NEXT?

LET'S HEAD SOUTH AND WARM UP A BIT! EAST OR WEST? YOU DECIDE.

FLY 8 HRS 30 MINS
GO TO **P122**

FLY 9 HRS 30 MINS
GO TO **P154**

ENJOY THE CALM OF...

KERALA!

THE STATE OF KERALA IN SOUTHERN INDIA IS BLESSED WITH
NATURAL BEAUTY. IF WE TAKE A SHORT TRIP INLAND FROM ITS
SUN-KISSED BEACHES, WE'LL DISCOVER A NETWORK OF RIVERS
THREADING THROUGH KERALA'S FORESTS. BUT BE WARY – BEYOND
THE PALM FORESTS AND COCONUT GROVES YOU MAY FIND PROWLING
BENGAL TIGERS, LEOPARDS, AND WILD ELEPHANTS!

THE ELEPHANT IS THE STATE ANIMAL OF KERALA AND OFTEN TAKES PART IN RELIGIOUS FESTIVALS.

WHERE NEXT?

LIFE IS EASY HERE, BUT IT'S TIME TO MAKE OUR WAY TO THE AIRPORT AT KOCHI.

FLY 9 HRS

GO TO P32

FLY 5 HRS 30 MINS

GO TO P88

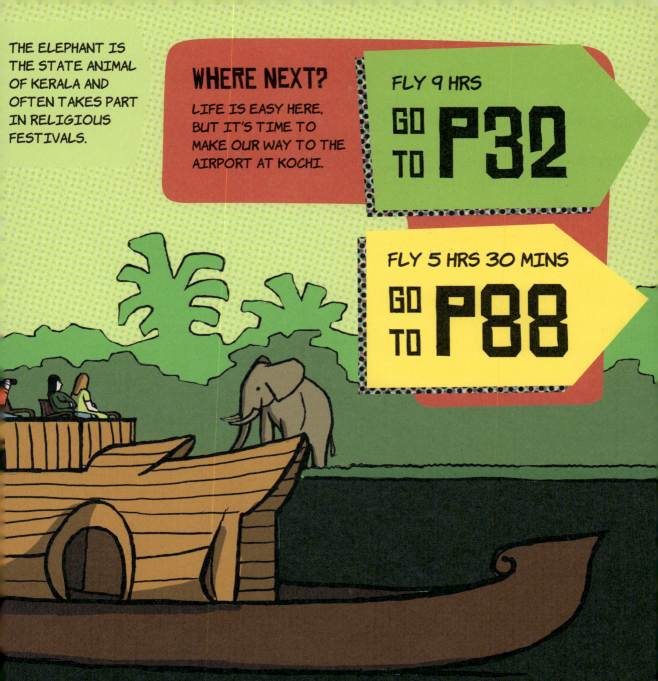

DRIFT ON A HOUSEBOAT

THE BEST WAY TO TAKE IT ALL IN IS ON BOARD ONE OF THE SIMPLE, WOODEN HOUSEBOATS, KNOWN LOCALLY AS KETTUVALLAMS, WHICH GLIDE GENTLY ALONG KERALA'S RIVERS, CANALS, AND LAGOONS. WE COULD EVEN GO DIVING FOR MUSSELS AND GIVE THEM TO THE CHEF TO COOK FOR DINNER. SCRUMMY!

SOAK UP THE SUN IN...
SYDNEY!

G'DAY! LET'S WANDER AROUND AUSTRALIA'S BIGGEST CITY AND THE CAPITAL OF NEW SOUTH WALES. A FUNKY METROPOLIS OF 4.5 MILLION PEOPLE, VISITORS COME FROM ALL OVER THE WORLD TO ENJOY THE CITY'S COOL, LAID-BACK LIFESTYLE. THERE'S SO MUCH TO DO! WE COULD GAZE INTO THE WORLD'S LARGEST NATURAL HARBOR FROM THE FAMOUS HARBOUR BRIDGE OR HAVE SOME FUN ON BONDI BEACH. HEY, DON'T FORGET YOUR SUNSCREEN – THE RAYS ARE STRONG HERE!

PEOPLE WHO LIVE IN SYDNEY ARE KNOWN AS SYDNEYSIDERS.

FLY 1 HR 30 MINS
GO TO P18

FLY 10 HRS
GO TO P54

SYDNEY OPERA HOUSE

SINCE IT OPENED IN 1973, THE OPERA HOUSE HAS BECOME A SYMBOL OF SYDNEY AND AUSTRALIA, TOO. IT WAS ACTUALLY DESIGNED BY A DANISH ARCHITECT, JØRN UTZON. MANY OF THE WORLD'S GREATEST MUSICIANS AND PERFORMERS HAVE APPEARED HERE OVER THE YEARS.

FLY 22 HRS 30 MINS
GO TO P70

WHERE NEXT?

IT'S TIME TO LEAVE BEHIND THE SUNSHINE, BONDI BEACH, AND THE BLUE MOUNTAINS...

FLY 21 HRS 30 MINS
GO TO P66

SINGAPORE!

WELCOME TO SINGAPORE – THE WORLD'S ONLY ISLAND CITY-STATE. THIS IS A PLACE WHERE PEOPLE COME FROM ALL OVER THE WORLD TO DO BUSINESS. OFFICE BUILDINGS, SHOPPING MALLS, AND LUXURY APARTMENTS SIT SIDE BY SIDE WITH TROPICAL FRUIT GROVES AND RAINFORESTS FILLED WITH CHATTERING MONKEYS. IT'S NOT CALLED "THE CITY IN A GARDEN" FOR NOTHING!

THE GARDEN BY THE BAY IS HOME TO 18 MAN-MADE SUPER-TREES. OVER 163,000 PLANTS AND FLOWERS GROW UP THESE GARDENS IN THE SKY!

MARINA BAY SANDS

WE MUST VISIT THE RECORD-BREAKING MARINA BAY SANDS RESORT, HOME TO SHOPS, A HOTEL, MUSEUMS, THEATERS, AND EVEN AN ICE RINK! THE THREE TOWERS THAT MAKE UP THE RESORT ARE TOPPED BY THE WORLD'S LARGEST SKY PARK, WHICH INCLUDES A 490 FT (150 M) INFINITY POOL OVERLOOKING THE CITY!

FLY 7 HRS 30 MINS
GO TO P18

FLY 4 HRS
GO TO P160

FLY 13 HRS 30 MINS
GO TO P66

WHERE NEXT?

LET'S SPEND OUR LAST FEW SINGAPORE DOLLARS BEFORE WE GO.

EDINBURGH!

THE SCOTTISH CAPITAL IS ONE GOOD-LOOKING CITY! TALL, ELEGANT BUILDINGS LINE IMPRESSIVELY WIDE STREETS LIKE THE ROYAL MILE AND PRINCES STREET. AND IT ALL SITS ON TOP OF A SERIES OF ROCKY HILLS THAT STARE OUT OVER THE SEA. IT'S THE PERFECT PLACE FOR GOING OUT AND ENJOYING YOURSELF, ESPECIALLY IN SUMMER, WHEN THE EDINBURGH ARTS FESTIVAL TAKES OVER THE WHOLE CITY FOR A MONTH!

IN 1824, EDINBURGH BECAME THE FIRST CITY IN THE WORLD TO HAVE ITS OWN FIRE DEPARTMENT!

EDINBURGH CASTLE

EDINBURGH'S MOST FAMOUS SIGHT WAS BUILT ON TOP OF AN EXTINCT VOLCANO! THE CASTLE IS A MIGHTY FORTRESS PERCHED HIGH ON CASTLE ROCK, KEEPING THE CITY SAFE FOR ALMOST 1,000 YEARS. IT USED TO BE HOME TO THE KINGS AND QUEENS OF SCOTLAND. LISTEN FOR THE EAR-SPLITTING SOUND OF THE ONE O'CLOCK GUN THAT IS FIRED EVERY AFTERNOON!

WHERE NEXT?

GOODBYE "AULD REEKIE" (EDINBURGH'S NICKNAME). IT'S TIME WE MOVED ON.

FLY 12 HRS 30 MINS
GO TO P82

FLY 2 HRS 30 MINS
GO TO P72

FLY 3 HRS
GO TO P100

VANCOUVER!

STANLEY PARK

HOW ABOUT A BIKE RIDE AROUND THE SPECTACULAR SEAWALL THAT CIRCLES THE CITY'S BEAUTIFUL STANLEY PARK? THERE'S NO BETTER WAY TO GLIMPSE THE CITY'S HARBOR AND COASTLINE, AND WE CAN KEEP AN EYE OUT FOR THE PARK'S FAMOUS TOTEM POLES, TOO. AFTER ALL THAT, WE'LL SKIP OVER TO TRENDY CHINATOWN FOR A DELICIOUS AND WELL-EARNED DINNER.

VANCOUVER IS THE BIGGEST CITY IN THE WESTERN CANADIAN PROVINCE OF BRITISH COLUMBIA. THIS IS A MODERN CITY SET AGAINST THE BACKDROP OF THE PACIFIC OCEAN ON ONE SIDE AND JAW-DROPPING MOUNTAINS ON THE OTHER! THERE AREN'T MANY PLACES WHERE YOU CAN PEEK THROUGH A CITYSCAPE OF GLASS TOWERS TO SEE SNOW-COVERED PEAKS ONLY A HALF-HOUR DRIVE AWAY. WHAT ARE WE WAITING FOR?

YOU CAN SAIL, SWIM, GOLF, KAYAK, AND SKI IN VANCOUVER – ALL ON THE SAME DAY. AND YOU COULD CYCLE ACROSS LIONS GATE BRIDGE!

FLY 10 HRS

GO TO P130

FLY 4 HRS 10 MINS

GO TO P112

WHERE NEXT?

THE PACIFIC NORTHWEST IS AMAZING, BUT WE NEED TO FLY EAST.

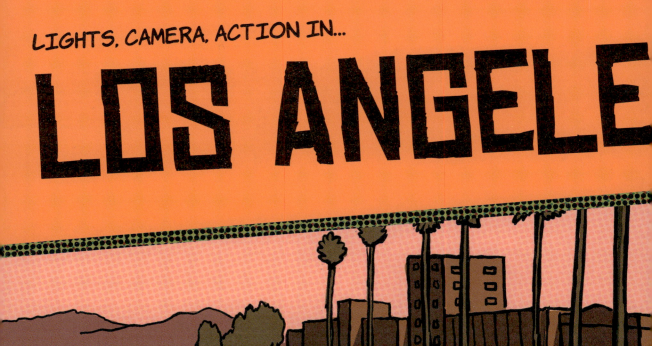

LIGHTS, CAMERA, ACTION IN...
LOS ANGELE

LET'S TAKE A LOOK AROUND LOS ANGELES, "THE CITY OF ANGELS." IT'S THE LARGEST CITY IN THE STATE OF CALIFORNIA AND IS FAMOUS FOR ITS BEAUTIFUL WEATHER, BEAUTIFUL BEACHES, AND BEAUTIFUL PEOPLE. IT'S THE ENTERTAINMENT CAPITAL OF THE WORLD AND HOME OF HOLLYWOOD, SO PREPARE TO BUMP INTO A STAR OR TWO AND RUB ELBOWS WITH FOLK FROM ALL OVER THE WORLD WHO HAVE COME HERE TO MAKE IT BIG IN THE MOVIES!

RODEO DRIVE

HOW ABOUT TAKING A TRIP ALONG RODEO DRIVE, THE FAMOUS STREET IN THE BEVERLEY HILLS NEIGHBORHOOD WHERE PEOPLE GO TO SEE AND BE SEEN? THERE ARE SOME SERIOUSLY EXPENSIVE SHOPS HERE, SELLING WHATEVER YOUR AVERAGE HOLLYWOOD MOVIE STAR DREAMS OF BUYING. DON'T FORGET TO BRING PLENTY OF SPENDING MONEY!

WHEN IT WAS FIRST PUT UP IN 1923, THE CITY'S LEGENDARY HOLLYWOOD SIGN ACTUALLY READ HOLLYWOODLAND.

WHERE NEXT?

PRESS PAUSE ON YOUR DREAMS OF BEING A MOVIE STAR! LET'S PACK AND HEAD TO LAX AIRPORT.

CATCH A PLANE
GO TO P80

DRIVE
GO TO P92

LA PAZ!

PREPARE TO HAVE YOUR BREATH TAKEN AWAY BY LA PAZ, CAPITAL OF BOLIVIA IN SOUTH AMERICA AND THE HIGHEST CITY IN THE WORLD. PERCHED HIGH IN THE ANDES MOUNTAINS, AT OVER 11,500 FT (3,500 M) ABOVE SEA LEVEL, YOU'LL BE GASPING FOR BREATH WHEN YOU ARRIVE. THE CITY ITSELF CLINGS TO THE SIDES OF A GIANT CANYON AND IS OVERLOOKED BY THE MIGHTY ILLIMANI MOUNTAIN. YOU'LL NEED YOUR CAMERA TO CAPTURE THE STUNNING VIEWS.

CITY IN THE SKY

THE BEST WAY TO SEE THE CITY IS WAY UP NEAR THE CLOUDS. WE'RE GOING TO TAKE A RIDE ON THE MI TELEFÉRICO, A NETWORK OF CABLE CARS THAT OPENED IN 2014 TO TAKE PASSENGERS BETWEEN LA PAZ AND THE NEIGHBORING CITY OF EL ALTO. HERE'S HOPING YOU HAVE A HEAD FOR HEIGHTS!

IF YOU'RE SUFFERING FROM ANY AILMENTS ON THIS JOURNEY, CHECK OUT THE WITCHES' MARKET IN LA PAZ – YOU'LL FIND A LOCAL POTION OR SPELL THERE THAT WILL CURE YOU.

WHERE NEXT?

WANT A FROG SMOOTHIE BEFORE WE GO TO THE AIRPORT? I'M NOT KIDDING!

FLY 21 HRS
GO TO **P104**

FLY 9 HRS
GO TO **P58**

PARIS!

AHH, PARIS — ROMANTIC, SOPHISTICATED, AND UNFORGETTABLE. WHAT SHALL WE DO FIRST? LINE UP TO SEE THE *MONA LISA* IN THE FAMOUS LOUVRE GALLERY? TAKE A RIVERBOAT RIDE ALONG THE SEINE? OR VISIT THE ARC DE TRIOMPHE AND NOTRE DAME? THERE'S REALLY ONLY ONE PLACE TO START OUR VISIT...

THE EIFFEL TOWER

FOR THE PERFECT VIEW, LET'S GO TO THE TOP OF THE EIFFEL TOWER — THE TALLEST BUILDING IN THE CITY. WE COULD TAKE THE ELEVATOR, BUT IT'S MORE FUN TO CLIMB THE STAIRS — ALMOST 2,000 OF THEM. DID YOU KNOW THAT GUSTAVE EIFFEL, WHO DESIGNED THE TOWER IN THE 1870S, ALSO BUILT THE STATUE OF LIBERTY IN NEW YORK CITY?

WHERE NEXT?

FAREWELL PARIS, IT WAS GOOD WHILE IT LASTED. UNTIL NEXT TIME!

FLY 11 HRS
GO TO **P116**

FLY 1 HR 15 MINS
DRIVE 30 MINS
GO TO **P10**

THE CATACOMBS

UNDERNEATH THE STREETS OF PARIS LIES A SERIES OF TUNNELS FILLED WITH THE SKELETONS OF 6 MILLION PEOPLE. THEY WERE MOVED THERE OVER TWO CENTURIES AGO BECAUSE THE GRAVEYARDS OF PARIS WERE FULL.

YOU'RE ON A
BIKE

IT'S TIME TO TRAVEL BY PEDAL POWER. THERE'S NOTHING QUITE LIKE THE FEELING OF FREEDOM YOU GET WHEN YOU HOP ON YOUR BICYCLE, PUT YOUR FEET ON THE PEDALS, AND GET GOING. IT'S JUST YOU, THE BIKE, AND THE OPEN ROAD. BUT REMEMBER TO WEAR A HELMET AND PACK A TIRE REPAIR KIT!

HORSELESS CARRIAGE

A GERMAN BARON CALLED KARL VON DRAIS INVENTED THE FIRST MODERN BICYCLE. IT WAS CALLED A HORSELESS CARRIAGE, AND ALTHOUGH IT HAD TWO WHEELS, THERE WERE NO PEDALS. THE RIDER MOVED ALONG BY PUSHING HIS FEET AGAINST THE GROUND!

THE WORLD'S LONGEST TANDEM BIKE HAS SEATS FOR 35 RIDERS!

WHERE NEXT?

WE'RE ALL SET FOR THE OPEN ROAD. HOW FAR WILL YOUR LEGS TAKE YOU?

CYCLE 13 HRS
GO TO P10

CYCLE 11 HRS
GO TO P62

LUXOR!

SAILING ALONG THE NILE

I'VE GOT US A COUPLE OF SEATS ON A FELUCCA
THAT WILL TAKE US ACROSS THE RIVER TO THE VALLEY OF THE KINGS.
FELUCCAS ARE THE TRADITIONAL WOODEN BOATS THAT HAVE SAILED THE
NILE FOR CENTURIES. UH OH! A NILE CROCODILE – RARE IN THIS PART OF THE
RIVER – HAS CRAWLED INTO THE WATER AND IS MAKING A BEELINE FOR OUR
BOAT! YIKES! WE'D BETTER TURN AROUND, AND FAST! BACK TO LONDON WE GO.
IT'S TIME TO START ALL OVER AGAIN.

LUXOR IS A MODERN EGYPTIAN CITY THAT LIES ON THE SITE OF THE ANCIENT CITY OF THEBES. IT'S CRAMMED WITH TEMPLES AND TOMBS THAT ARE THOUSANDS OF YEARS OLD. A SHORT HOP ACROSS THE RIVER NILE (THE WORLD'S LONGEST RIVER) WILL TAKE US TO THE VALLEY OF THE KINGS, THE LEGENDARY BURIAL PLACE OF THE PHARAOHS OF ANCIENT EGYPT!

THE TOMB OF THE PHARAOH TUTANKHAMUN WAS DISCOVERED IN THE VALLEY OF THE KINGS IN 1925. HIS DEATH MASK IS MADE OF PURE GOLD!

DEAD END!

EXPLORE EXOTIC...

KATHMANDU!

NEPAL IS THE ONLY COUNTRY IN THE WORLD WITH A FLAG THAT ISN'T RECTANGULAR. IT'S THE COLOR OF THE RED RHODODENDRON, THE NATIONAL FLOWER OF NEPAL, AND SHOWS A SUN AND A CRESCENT MOON.

KATHMANDU IS A RIOT OF COLORS, SMELLS, AND SOUNDS, BUT DON'T WORRY, WE'LL CHECK OUT SOME OF ITS QUIETER CORNERS, TOO. AWAY FROM THE STREETS TEEMING WITH BACKPACKING TOURISTS AND GUESTHOUSES, THERE ARE BEAUTIFUL OLD BUDDHIST AND HINDU TEMPLES, AND CHILES DRYING IN ANCIENT SQUARES.

DURBAR SQUARE

LET'S HEAD TO THE OLD TOWN AND DURBAR SQUARE, HOME TO MEDIEVAL ROYAL PALACES AND TEMPLES. LOOK FOR THE SADHUS (HOLY MEN), WITH THEIR BRIGHT ROBES, LONG BEARDS, AND COLORFUL FACE PAINT. IF WE'RE FEELING HUNGRY, THERE'S BOUND TO BE A STREET VENDOR COOKING MOMOS — TASTY STEAMED DUMPLINGS SERVED WITH A SPICY CHILE SAUCE.

WHERE NEXT?

THERE'S ONLY ONE WAY OUT OF THIS CITY FOR US AND THAT'S BY ROAD.

GO TO P20

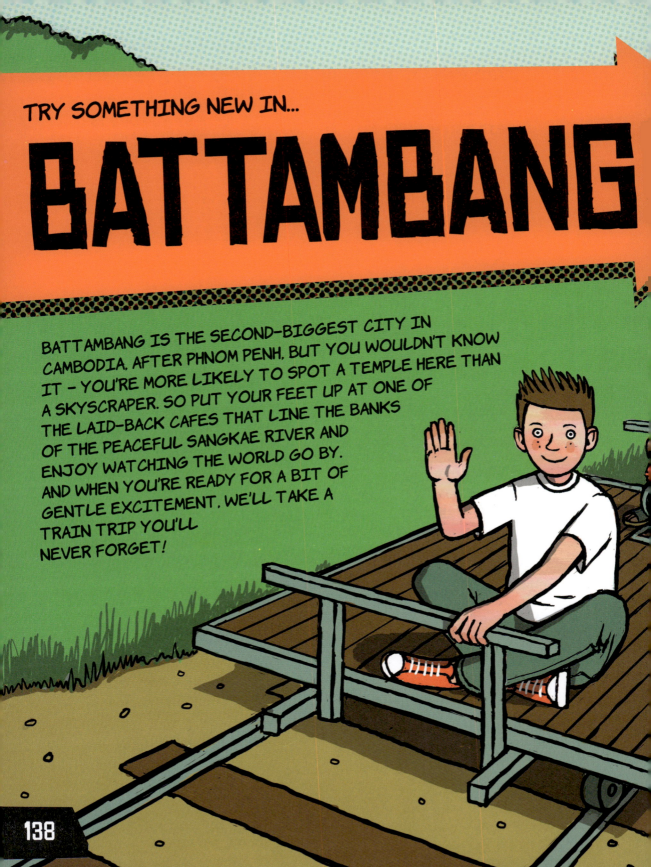

TRY SOMETHING NEW IN...

BATTAMBANG

BATTAMBANG IS THE SECOND-BIGGEST CITY IN CAMBODIA, AFTER PHNOM PENH, BUT YOU WOULDN'T KNOW IT – YOU'RE MORE LIKELY TO SPOT A TEMPLE HERE THAN A SKYSCRAPER. SO PUT YOUR FEET UP AT ONE OF THE LAID-BACK CAFES THAT LINE THE BANKS OF THE PEACEFUL SANGKAE RIVER AND ENJOY WATCHING THE WORLD GO BY. AND WHEN YOU'RE READY FOR A BIT OF GENTLE EXCITEMENT, WE'LL TAKE A TRAIN TRIP YOU'LL NEVER FORGET!

TRADITIONALLY, CAMBODIANS DO NOT CELEBRATE THEIR BIRTHDAYS!

WHERE NEXT?

THE CLOSEST AIRPORT IS AT SIEM REAP, BUT FIRST WE HAVE TO DRIVE...

DRIVE 2 HRS FLY 1 HR

GO TO P90

DRIVE 2 HRS FLY 3 HRS

GO TO P46

ALL ABOARD THE BAMBOO TRAIN

THE BATTAMBANG BAMBOO TRAIN IS A TRAIN JOURNEY LIKE NO OTHER! THE TINY, RICKETY TRAINS, KNOWN AS NORRIES BY THE LOCALS, USED TO TRANSPORT GOODS INCLUDING CATTLE AND PIGS, BUT NOWADAYS YOU'RE MORE LIKELY TO SEE PEOPLE ON BOARD. THERE'S ONLY ONE TRACK, SO IF WE APPROACH A NORRIE COMING THE OPPOSITE WAY, THE DRIVER OF THE LESS-BUSY NORRIE HAS TO TAKE HIS VEHICLE APART AND PUT IT BACK TOGETHER WHEN THE OTHER HAS PASSED!

BUSTLE AROUND...
BEIJING!

THE GREAT WALL

LET'S BE SURE TO VISIT THE GREAT WALL OF CHINA WHILE WE'RE HERE — ONE OF THE MOST FAMOUS CONSTRUCTIONS IN THE WORLD. WORK BEGAN ON THESE AMAZING FORTIFICATIONS AROUND 770 BC, AND THE WALLS STRETCH FOR THOUSANDS OF MILES. WE COULD GO TO THE SECTION AT MUTIANYU, AND TAKE A CHAIRLIFT UP TO THE TOP, THEN RIDE A WHEELED TOBOGGAN BACK DOWN!

BEIJING, THE CAPITAL CITY OF CHINA, IS ALWAYS REINVENTING ITSELF, LOOKING TO THE FUTURE EVEN AS IT VALUES ITS HISTORY. NO SURPRISE THEN THAT INCREDIBLE MODERN BUILDINGS LIKE THE OLYMPIC STADIUM, NICKNAMED "THE BIRD'S NEST," SIT ALONGSIDE UNFORGETTABLE OLD MONUMENTS SUCH AS THE FORBIDDEN CITY, A GIANT ROYAL PALACE.

WHERE NEXT?

LET'S SPEND OUR LAST FEW RENMINBI ON A BOWL OF NOODLES BEFORE WE GO.

FLY 11 HRS
GO TO P100

FLY 3 HRS 30 MINS
GO TO P160

FLY 4 HRS 30 MINS
GO TO P90

BUILDERS ON THE GREAT WALL USED STICKY RICE TO GLUE ITS BRICKS AND STONES TOGETHER!

DARJEELING

DARJEELING IS A SPECTACULAR TOWN IN THE INDIAN STATE OF WEST BENGAL. SITTING ON A HIMALAYAN MOUNTAIN RIDGE, IT'S THE PERFECT PLACE TO ESCAPE THE BLAZING SUMMER HEAT IN THE VALLEY BELOW. WE'LL GET UP EARLY AND HEAD FOR TIGER HILL TO WATCH THE SUN RISE OVER KANGCHENJUNGA, THE WORLD'S THIRD-HIGHEST MOUNTAIN, THEN HEAD BACK TO TOWN FOR A REFRESHING CUP OF DARJEELING'S WORLD-FAMOUS TEA.

HIMALAYAN RAILWAY

THE MOST FUN WAY TO GET UP TO DARJEELING IS ON THE DARJEELING HIMALAYAN RAILWAY, WHICH HAS BEEN TRANSPORTING VISITORS SINCE 1881 BECAUSE IT RUNS ON A THIN SET OF RAILS ONLY TWO FEET WIDE. IT'S SOMETIMES CALLED THE TOY TRAIN. IT MIGHT BE DINKY, BUT THE VIEWS YOU'LL SEE ON THE WAY UP WILL LEAVE YOU SPEECHLESS!

THE MOST EXPENSIVE TEA EVER SOLD COMES FROM DARJEELING. IN 2014, A SINGLE KILOGRAM COST $2200!

WHERE NEXT?

WE'LL HAVE TO RENT A CAR OR TAKE A TAXI FOR THE THREE-HOUR DRIVE DOWN THE MOUNTAINS TO THE NEAREST AIRPORT. THEN...

FLY 4 HRS
GO TO P36

FLY 2 HRS
GO TO P88

BULLET TRAIN

LET'S FACE IT, TRAVELING BY TRAIN CAN BE SLOW AND BORING. THAT'S NOT A PROBLEM IN JAPAN, WHERE SO-CALLED "BULLET" TRAINS FLY ALONG A NETWORK OF HIGH-SPEED LINES KNOWN AS THE SHINKANSEN, TRAVELING AT SPEEDS OF 200 MI (320 KM) PER HOUR. THE FIRST OF THESE LINES OPENED IN 1964, CARRYING PASSENGERS BETWEEN THE CITIES OF TOKYO AND OSAKA.

MOUNT FUJI

LET'S TAKE THE SHINKANSEN FROM TOKYO, AND WE'LL CATCH A GLIMPSE OF MOUNT FUJI, OR "FUJI-SAN" AS IT'S KNOWN HERE. THIS ACTIVE VOLCANO IS JAPAN'S HIGHEST MOUNTAIN AND IT'S ONE OF THREE SACRED MOUNTAINS IN THE COUNTRY.

EVERY BULLET TRAIN REACHES ITS DESTINATION WITHIN A MINUTE OF ITS SCHEDULED ARRIVAL TIME!

WHERE NEXT?

YOUR TRAIN IS NONSTOP, SO THERE'S ONLY ONE CHOICE HERE.

TRAVEL 2 HRS 20 MINS

GO TO P94

KICK BACK IN...

KINGSTON!

COME EXPLORE KINGSTON, THE CAPITAL OF THE ISLAND OF JAMAICA. IT'S A MAGICAL SETTING, SNUGGLED BETWEEN THE BLUE MOUNTAINS AND A HUGE NATURAL HARBOR. WE CAN SAMPLE THE SIZZLING JERK CHICKEN, A SPICY LOCAL TREAT.

BOB MARLEY, THE MOST FAMOUS REGGAE SINGER WHO EVER LIVED, GREW UP IN KINGSTON.

THERE'S A BAND HERE PLAYING
JAMAICA'S OWN SPECIAL MUSIC,
CALLED REGGAE. YOUR REGGAE MOVES
ARE SO GROOVY THAT THE BASS PLAYER
ASKS IF YOU'D LIKE TO BE A BACKING
DANCER ON THEIR TOUR!

YOU AGREE, SO IT'S BACK TO LONDON
FOR YOU FOR THE FIRST GIG. TRY THIS
TRIP AGAIN ONCE THE SHOW IS OVER.
SEE YOU ON STAGE!

DEAD END!

ENJOY THE VIEW IN...

VICTORIA!

HERE WE ARE IN THE PINT-SIZED CAPITAL OF THE SEYCHELLES, A COUNTRY MADE UP OF 115 SEPARATE ISLANDS IN THE INDIAN OCEAN. WE ARE ON MAHÉ, THE BIGGEST ISLAND, BUT LET'S TAKE TIME TO EXPLORE SOME OF THE OTHERS. TURQUOISE SEAS, WHITE SANDY BEACHES, LUSH JUNGLE, AND STUNNING SUNSETS ARE WAITING. THIS IS THE STUFF OF DREAMS.

RUMOR HAS IT THAT THE TREASURE OF INFAMOUS PIRATE OLIVIER LEVASSEUR REMAINS BURIED SOMEWHERE IN THE SEYCHELLES. PACK A SHOVEL!

WHERE NEXT?

IT'S SO HARD TO LEAVE, BUT TIME WAITS FOR NO ONE, SO LET'S GET GOING.

FLY 5 HRS

GO TO P96

FLY 9 HRS 45 MINS

GO TO P140

COCO DE MER

WE'RE TAKING A FERRY TO PRASLIN, ANOTHER ISLAND, WHERE WE'LL EXPLORE THE VALLÉE DE MAI. THIS IS AN AREA OF DENSE FOREST WHERE COCO DE MER PALM TREES GROW. THIS PALM ONLY GROWS ON TWO ISLANDS AND IT PRODUCES THE BIGGEST AND HEAVIEST SEEDS IN THE PLANT KINGDOM! IF WE'RE LUCKY, WE'LL CATCH A GLIMPSE OF THE RARE BLUE PIGEON, TOO.

BERLIN!

GUTEN TAG – GOOD DAY – FROM GERMANY'S ENERGETIC CAPITAL CITY. FOUNDED IN 1237, BERLIN'S STORY HAS NOT ALWAYS BEEN A HAPPY ONE. IN THE 20TH CENTURY, LARGE PARTS WERE DESTROYED IN THE SECOND WORLD WAR, AND THEN THE CITY WAS DIVIDED IN TWO. BUT SINCE GERMANY WAS REUNITED IN 1989, BERLIN HAS BECOME A COOL, CREATIVE, MODERN METROPOLIS. WHATEVER THE HOUR OF DAY OR NIGHT, THERE IS ALWAYS SOMETHING EXCITING TO DO OR SEE.

A BERLINER IS NOT ONLY SOMEONE WHO LIVES IN THE CITY BUT ALSO A TYPE OF DOUGHNUT!

WHERE NEXT?

IT'S GOODBYE, OR *AUF WIEDERSEHEN* AS THEY SAY IN BERLIN. SHALL WE FLY EAST OR SOUTH?

EAST 2 HRS 30 MINS
GO TO P22

SOUTH 2 HRS 30 MINS
GO TO P70

THE BERLIN WALL

BERLINERS ARE CAREFUL NOT TO FORGET THE PAST, SO LET'S CHECK OUT THE REMAINS OF THE BERLIN WALL ON BERNAUER STRASSE. FOR 28 YEARS FROM 1961, THE WALL PREVENTED THE RESIDENTS OF EAST AND WEST BERLIN FROM CROSSING FROM ONE SIDE TO THE OTHER. THIS WAS BECAUSE THE COMMUNIST RULERS OF EAST GERMANY WANTED TO CONTROL ITS CITIZENS. THE DAY THE WALL WAS TORN DOWN WAS ONE OF THE HAPPIEST DAYS IN GERMAN HISTORY.

SETTLE DOWN ON A...
SLOW BOAT

THE MODERN WORLD IS A FAST-MOVING PLACE, SO AFTER FLYING TO CHIANG RAI IN NORTHERN THAILAND, IT'S GREAT TO HAVE A CHANGE OF PACE. LET'S TRAVEL THE WAY THE LOCALS DO – BY BUS AND SLOW BOAT. FORGET ABOUT THE TIME AS WE CRUISE ON THE MEKONG AND MAE KOK – ASIA'S MIGHTY RIVER HIGHWAYS. SPEED ISN'T ON THE AGENDA HERE. WE'LL GET TO OUR DESTINATION WHEN WE GET THERE, AND NOT A MINUTE BEFORE.

THE WORLD'S LONGEST CRUISE LASTS 357 DAYS. HOPEFULLY, EVEN OUR SLOW BOAT WILL BE QUICKER THAN THAT!

SAIL 5 HRS, DRIVE 3 HRS

GO TO P12

WHERE NEXT?

LET'S LOSE TRACK OF TIME AND LET THE WORLD DRIFT BY FOR A WHILE.

DRIVE 1 DAY, SAIL 2 DAYS

GO TO P76

GET COMFY

I'VE RESERVED TICKETS ON AN OLD CONVERTED CARGO SHIP. WE'LL BE SITTING ON WOODEN BENCHES, BUT REMEMBER, THESE VESSELS WEREN'T MADE TO CARRY PEOPLE, SO DON'T EXPECT TO BE TOO COMFORTABLE. MY ADVICE IS TO BRING A CUSHION AND A GOOD BOOK. YOU'LL HAVE PLENTY OF TIME TO READ IT!

VISIT WINTER WONDERLAND IN...
LAPLAND!

HOLD ON TIGHT AS WE ZIP ALONG THE SURFACE OF THE SNOW. KEEP AN EYE OUT FOR WILD REINDEER, WOLVES, LYNX, OR EVEN BEARS. AND MAYBE WE'LL SEE SANTA CLAUS! SOME PEOPLE SAY HE LIVES UP HERE IN FROZEN LAPLAND.

YOU'VE MADE IT TO THE FAR NORTH OF FINLAND! LET'S EXPLORE THIS WINTER WONDERLAND BY TRYING OUR HAND AT DOG SLEDDING. A TEAM OF HUSKIES WILL PULL US ALONG, THROUGH A LANDSCAPE OF FROZEN LAKES AND SNOW-DUSTED FIR TREES.

UH OH! THE SLED SKIDS AROUND A TIGHT CORNER AND TOPPLES INTO A SNOWDRIFT. WORSE STILL, ALL THE HUSKIES HAVE RUN OFF! THIS IS THE END OF THE ROAD FOR YOU, I'M AFRAID. RETURN TO LONDON AND START AGAIN.

DEAD END!

HUSKIES CAN WITHSTAND TEMPERATURES AS COLD AS −58°F (−50°C).

IT'S A WONDERFUL TOWN...
NEW YORK!

WELCOME TO THE BIG APPLE – THE BIGGEST CITY IN THE US. THEY SAY THAT NEW YORK NEVER SLEEPS, AND IT'S TRUE THAT THERE IS ALWAYS SOMETHING TO DO HERE, 24 HOURS A DAY. WALKING THROUGH THIS CITY FEELS LIKE BEING ON A FILM SET. YOU'RE SURE TO HAVE SEEN LOTS OF ITS MOST FAMOUS SIGHTS IN THE MOVIES – THE STATUE OF LIBERTY, THE EMPIRE STATE BUILDING, BROOKLYN BRIDGE, TIMES SQUARE, CENTRAL PARK – THE LIST GOES ON!

NEW YORK WAS ORIGINALLY RULED BY THE DUTCH, WHO CALLED IT NEW AMSTERDAM.

WHERE NEXT?

HOLD ON TO YOUR DOLLARS. YOU MAY STILL NEED THEM.

TAKE A TRAIN
GO TO **P124**

CATCH A PLANE
GO TO **P18**

TAKE A BUS
GO TO **P78**

YELLOW CAB

LET'S HEAD FOR CENTRAL PARK. WE'LL HAIL ONE OF THE FAMOUS CANARY-YELLOW TAXICABS TO TAKE US THERE. AND IF WE ASK NICELY, PERHAPS OUR DRIVER WILL STOP TO LET US PICK UP AN AUTHENTIC NEW YORK HOT DOG ON THE WAY!

CLOSE ENCOUNTERS NEAR...
MAUN!

HERE WE ARE IN MAUN, A SMALL TOWN IN THE AFRICAN NATION OF BOTSWANA. THERE ARE LOTS OF AMAZING TRADITIONAL VILLAGES CLOSE BY. LIKE MOST VISITORS, WE'LL USE THE TOWN AS A BASE AND EXPLORE THE VAST GRASSY RIVER PLAINS OF THE OKAVANGO DELTA, HOME TO MUCH OF BOTSWANA'S AWESOME WILDLIFE.

BOTSWANA HAS MORE ELEPHANTS THAN ANY OTHER COUNTRY, AND MORE MEERKATS, TOO!

WHERE NEXT?

WE'LL COME BACK TO BOTSWANA ONE DAY, BUT NOW, IT'S TIME TO GO.

FLY 15 HRS 30 MINS
GO TO P50

FLY 20 HRS
GO TO P82

SELINDA SPILLWAY

WE'RE GOING TO TAKE A SHORT FLIGHT AND THEN PICK UP A LONG CANADIAN CANOE TO PADDLE DOWN THE SELINDA SPILLWAY. THIS PLACE IS FULL OF RIVERS AND WETLANDS, AND THERE'S A GOOD CHANCE WE'LL SPY CROCODILES, GIRAFFES, LIONS, AND EVEN ELEPHANTS. AT THE END OF THE DAY, WE'LL HEAD FOR CAMP AND DIG INTO A TASTY DINNER AROUND A BLAZING CAMPFIRE.

HOP A FERRY IN...

HONG KONG!

HONG KONG IS PART OF CHINA. BUT THIS CITY FEELS
VERY DIFFERENT FROM THE REST OF THE COUNTRY. IT
WAS A BRITISH COLONY FOR OVER 150 YEARS UNTIL 1997
AND BECAME AN IMPORTANT PLACE TO DO BUSINESS IN
ASIA. HONG KONG BECAME VERY RICH, AS YOU CAN SEE
FROM ALL THE SKYSCRAPERS. FOLLOW ME, AND I'LL SHOW
YOU WHERE BRITISH AND CHINESE CULTURES MEET! LOTS
OF THE NEIGHBORHOODS HAVE ENGLISH NAMES, AND WE
CAN HAVE AMAZING CHINESE FOOD FOR DINNER – YOU CAN
EVEN ORDER FRESH SNAKE IF YOU WANT – TASSSSSSSTY!

STAR FERRY

WE'RE ON A MOONLIT TRIP ON THE FAMOUS STAR FERRY THAT CROSSES VICTORIA HARBOUR BETWEEN HONG KONG ISLAND AND KOWLOON. THE SERVICE STARTED IN 1888 AND IS THE PERFECT WAY TO TAKE IN THE AMAZING SKYLINE AND WATCH THE AWESOME LIGHT SHOW THAT HAPPENS EVERY NIGHT IN THE SKY ABOVE THE BUILDINGS OF THE HARBOR.

WHERE NEXT?

CHEP LAK KOK AIRPORT IS 25 MI (40 KM) FROM THE CITY. LET'S TAKE A SHUTTLE BUS.

FLY 8 HRS
GO TO P84

FLY 2 HRS 30 MINS
GO TO P46

FLY 13 HRS 15 MINS
GO TO P134

HONG KONG'S NAME MEANS "FRAGRANT HARBOR." MAYBE IT'S BECAUSE THE HARBOR WATERS WERE THOUGHT TO BE SWEET-TASTING OR BECAUSE INCENSE WAS PRODUCED NEARBY.

ACKNOWLEDGEMENTS

PUBLISHING DIRECTOR
COMMISSIONING EDITORS

EDITOR
ASSISTANT EDITOR
AUTHOR
ARTIST
ART DIRECTOR
DESIGNER
PRINT PRODUCTION

PIERS PICKARD
JEN FEROZE,
CATHARINE ROBERTSON
JACQUELINE MCCANN
CHRISTINA WEBB
DAN SMITH
FRANCES CASTLE
ANDY MANSFIELD
KIM HANKINSON
LARISSA FROST,
NIGEL LONGUET

PUBLISHED IN FEBRUARY 2018 BY
LONELY PLANET GLOBAL LIMITED
CRN 554153
ISBN 978 1 78657 756 6
WWW.LONELYPLANETKIDS.COM
© LONELY PLANET 2018

10 9 8 7 6 5 4 3 2 1

PRINTED IN MALAYSIA

LONELY PLANET OFFICES

AUSTRALIA
THE MALT STORE, LEVEL 3, 551 SWANSTON ST,
CARLTON, VICTORIA 3053
T: 03 8379 8000

IRELAND
UNIT E, DIGITAL COURT, THE DIGITAL HUB,
RAINSFORD ST, DUBLIN 8

USA
124 LINDEN ST, OAKLAND, CA 94607
T: 510 250 6400

UK
240 BLACKFRIARS RD, LONDON SE1 8NW
T: 020 3771 5100

STAY IN TOUCH
LONELYPLANET.COM/CONTACT